From Language
To Communication

Second Edition

LEA's COMMUNICATION SERIES
Jennings Bryant/Dolf Zillmann, General Editors

For a complete list of other titles in LEA's Communication Series, please contact Lawrence Erlbaum Associates, Publishers.

From Language To Communication

Second Edition

Donald G. Ellis
University of Hartford

LAWRENCE ERLBAUM ASSOCIATES, PUBLISHERS
1999   Mahwah, New Jersey   London

Lawrence Erlbaum Associates, Inc., Publishers
10 Industrial Avenue
Mahwah, NJ 07430

Cover design by Kathryn Houghtaling Lacey

Library of Congress Cataloging-in-Publication Data

Ellis, Donald G.
From language to communication / Donald G. Ellis. —
2nd. ed.
    p. cm.
Includes bibliographical references and index.
ISBN 0-8058-3031-6 (cloth : alk. paper). —
ISBN 0-8058-3032-4 (pbk : alk. paper)
1. Language and languages. 2. Linguistics. 3. Communi-
cation. I. Title.
P106.E443 1999
  302.2—dc21   99-28859
                                         CIP

Books published by Lawrence Erlbaum Associates are printed
on acid-free paper, and their bindings are chosen for strength
and durability.

Printed in the United States of America
10 9 8 7 6 5 4 3 2 1

For
Florence and David Ellis
and
Karen, David, and Allie

Contents

Introduction

This book grew out of my conviction that language is the fundamental tool of communication and experience. The study of language has always been inherently fascinating to me. Unfortunately, too much of it is either written for scholars who have specialized training or overly popularized and simplistic. The aim of this book is to strike the middle ground.

I think the first edition of *From Language to Communication* successfully outlined basic issues in the relation between language and communication. It introduced students to elementary concepts in linguistics and then applied these concepts to interaction processes. This second edition updates much of that work and adds many topics that were not included in the first edition. Every chapter has been rewritten, some of them quite extensively, and chapter 8 is new. I have tried to make this edition of the book even more accessible to the introductory reader. There are many more examples, and I have worked hard to improve the readability of the book.

In this book, I am concerned with language issues of many kinds, but not all kinds. Language and the linguistic system that we learn are fundamentally a part of the communication process. As such, this volume includes significant issues in the study of language and communication that represent a perspective—a standpoint from which to view the field of study. I should say something more about the view from my particular standpoint.

Communication is a misunderstood discipline. The term *communication* can conjure up such diverse images as telephones, computers, television, intimate relations, the Internet, radio, and public speaking. All of these are in one way or another communicative. But using symbols to constitute and interpret reality is an essential feature of each. The technology of computers, television, and telephones make it possible for messages to reach larger numbers of us at greater distances more quickly. The sheer amount and variety of language we are exposed to has increased dramatically in the past decades. But whether a message is fashioned from the grunts of two cavemen arguing over a bone or finds its way into your living room after passing through computers and a short voyage in space, that message uses symbols to establish meaning.

Language has both form and strategy. This means it has both stable elements that are building blocks of messages and psychological and sociological influences that shape how language is used. The *form* of language is concerned with structures and rules for organizing these building blocks. Chapter 2 deals with the most basic of these rules, namely, sound rules, word formation rules, and syntactical structures. There are also structures of interaction sequences and rules for activities such as initiating and terminating conversations (chaps. 5 and 7), as well as larger structures for organizing entire stories and texts (chap. 6). A good portion of this book is devoted to these principles.

The *strategic* use of language focuses on how communication is used to achieve a purpose or goal. Any time a person thinks about their language and its effect on another person and chooses their language accordingly, they are thinking strategically about language. Politicians, advertisers, and lovers all think very carefully and strategically about the potential impact of their messages. There are also principles and patterns of strategic language use. These are more fluid and changing than structural rules, but knowledge of these strategic patterns still provides tools and resources for communicators to draw on. Sections of chapters 4, 5, 6, 7, and 8 pertain to strategic language.

There is no unified theory of language and communication, and I make little progress toward such a goal in this volume. Instead, I present language and communication as a series of topics that have some connections. I organized this volume as a movement from specific issues in language (linguistic traditions) to topics more generally concerned with the orderliness of communication. The final chapter (chap. 8) on sociolinguistics is the most broadly and socially conceived chapter in the book; hence, the title *From Language to Communication*. In one sense, the title is misleading because I do not mean to imply that language is prior to communication or can be separated from it. On the contrary, communication is the only function of language, and even abstract linguistic structures serve the communicative nature of language. The title reflects the presentation of topics in the book and is consistent with my decisions about how to segment the subject matter.

The book focuses on both the structure of texts and on some social and psychological aspects of language (especially chap. 8). It is important that individuals achieve *textuality* when communicating, or the sense that language is alive and performing some desired function. Language has achieved textuality when it is an instance of meaning. I have tried to present the current and interesting thinking on these subjects. The volume overview issues in linguistics, cognition, pragmatics, discourse, and semantics as they coalesce to create the communicative experience. These things are the carpentry out of which communication is built.

I very much want students to have an understanding of the relation between language and communication. A teacher receives a great deal from students, if only he or she lets it in. I have learned much from my students, and their questions, observations, and confusions have sharpened my own thinking. As a tribute to them, I have included their examples and concerns as frequently as possible. My scholarly, pedagogical, and personal goals will have been met if, on completion of this book, the reader feels as if he or she has a sense of key issues in the history and nature of language and how language works to stitch together a text that is an instance of social meaning.

I feel honored to have had the opportunity to revise this book and keep it alive. I am always grateful to my friends and colleagues in the School of Communication at the University of Hartford. We share that easy weave of personal friendship and professional life. I also want to thank the university for a sabbatical in the spring of 1998 that allowed me to finish the book. I spent most of that sabbatical in Israel, which is an energizing environment that fosters work and commitment. All of the people at Lawrence Erlbaum Associates have been very helpful and supportive. In particular, Linda Bathgate is a special person who was in no small way responsible for this volume.

Above all, my family always deserves recognition, especially my wife Karen. Her high standards of taste and clarity are valuable resources for author and husband. Finally, David and Allie always deepen my sense of continuity and connectedness. These, too, make for good people and good books.

—Donald G. Ellis

CHAPTER ONE

The Nature of Language: From Magic to Semantics

Even in the Bible, there are stories about the power of language. In Judges 12:1–7, it tells about the Gileadites, who were fighting the Ephraimites near the Jordan River. Whenever someone from Ephraim tried to cross the Jordan, the Gileadites would say, "Pronounce the word *shibboleth*." If the poor person trying to cross said "*sibboleth*," not pronouncing the word the way the Gileadites did, he was seized and killed by the banks of the Jordan River; 42,000 Ephraimites fell. This story certainly illustrates the potential power of language. People use the way you speak to draw conclusions about who you are, and they act on those conclusions. Language "marks" your identity and is the most important communication tool you have.

This book is about language and its relation to human communication. Many people believe that language is what makes humans unique. It is what gives us great mental powers. We explore in this volume the specific nature of language and how humans use it. We sample significant issues in language and communication and show how these are related to psychology, sociology, and linguistics.

When you speak English—or any other language—you are using a system of sounds that have developed and evolved over a long period of time. The language you learned growing up is called a *natural language*. In other words, it is not an artificial language or one made up by humans for computers, machines, or some special purpose. Natural human languages are very technical and governed by rules (see, e.g., chaps. 2 and 3), but on the other hand, natural languages are sensitive to people and the communities they live in.

Another way to say this is that languages have both structure and function. *Structure* is concerned with language as a specific and unique system of

1

sounds that have meanings. It is also concerned with the sequential organization of words, which is called *syntax*. The structure of a language is more formal and either never changes or changes very slowly. Most people do not know very much about language structure. Just as you can drive a car without understanding what is going on under the hood of the car, you can speak a language without understanding very much about how language works. Linguists usually study the structure of a language (e.g., Chomsky, 1966). They want to know what things are common to all languages and what principles govern how a language system works. Chapters 2 and 3 focus more on these issues.

A functional approach to language is much more interested in how people *use* language. Functionalists are more oriented toward communication and do not care very much about abstract rules. They would never separate language from the people who are using the language (e.g., Hymes, 1974). Most of this book is devoted to approaches more in line with functionalism than structuralism. As people interested in communication, we want to know how language works. We want to know how to create new meanings, express ourselves well, recognize when we are being manipulated, and to know what language tells us about people and their thoughts. If you listened to or read President Clinton's speech apologizing for his relationship with Monica Lewinsky, you listened to someone who was using language in complex strategic ways. The language had to serve as an apology but not appear too weak, it had to be careful of legal considerations but also sound genuine, it had to reassure the public and be respectful of his family. Crafting this sort of language requires a keen sense of how language functions and how it can be used for specific purposes.

The title *From Language to Communication* is intended to imply the mutuality of both "language" and "communication." Neither has the more important role in studying social interaction. In fact, the definitions of each imply the other; that is, any definition of language must include a communicative function, and it is equally impossible to define communication without reference to a linguistic component. But it is communication that provides the more general frame of reference. Language serves communication. Language is only useful or practical to the extent that it ministers to communicative goals. The aim of understanding communication in any culture is to clarify and keep in view the relations between messages and contexts. Let us begin with some orientation toward the historical treatment of language.

ORIGINS OF LANGUAGE

Early theories of language were preoccupied with its origins. Before the 18th century, theories attributed the origins of language to divine intervention. Language was considered a gift from God. Most cultures have a story or myth about the creation of language and the nature of the first language. In the Judeo-Christian tradition, Hebrew was the language of the Garden of Eden. Andreas Kemke, a 17th-century Swedish philologist, boldly claimed that Swedish was spoken in the Garden of Eden. Other cultures have creation stories that include the origin of language. The Egyptians are the oldest race and maintain that Egyptian was the original language. One of their ancient stories is about a ruler who removed children from their home at birth and placed them with shepherds who were ordered not to speak to babies. The story has it that the children spontaneously uttered Egyptian words at about the age of 2. This presumably proved that Egyptian was the original language.

All cultures have a language origin story. Although the facts of the story are irrelevant and certainly apocryphal, the existence of the stories and the elements they share are interesting. The sun goddess, Amaterasu, was the creator of language in Japan. In China, the Son of Heaven was T'ien-tzu, and he gave language and the power of words to man. Creation myths almost always have a god from the heavens or the god of light both creating man and giving him speech powers. These tendencies are recurring in the creation myths of the American Indians. Michabo was the god of light in Algonquian mythology, and the culture god of the Iroquois was the god of the dawn. From these collections of stories and myths come reports of similar experiences and behaviors. It is possible to interpret the myths as saying that language accompanied reason. The metaphor of light is typically associated with "knowledge" and "understanding," and it seems to be no accident that theories of the origin of language would accompany beliefs about when intelligent human behavior began. It must have been impossible for the ancients to conceive of human life without language, so language must have coincided with the birth of human beings.

Plato marks the beginning of the serious considerations about language. Early myths, including the Genesis story, simply stated the fact that language existed and a god gave it to man. In Genesis, it was the power to name things that God bestowed upon us. The author of the Genesis story provided no analysis or exposition of the history and nature of language. Plato, on the other hand, accepted the facts of language as given and then asked: "How did language come about?" or "What was the principle that guided the making of the first words?" Plato's approach was radical for its time and his analysis in the *Cratylus* is a combination of philosophy and science. Although Plato and the Greeks were somewhat vague about the origin of language, at least they were not mystical about it. Socrates, who does the talking about language in the *Cratylus*, reports that some words were not of Greek origin and must have been borrowed from their barbarian neighbors. The word *barbaros* in Greek implies "babbler" and certainly suggests what the Greeks must have thought about their own language compared to others. Socrates reasons that because barbarians were an older race that came before the Greeks (more primitive of course), it would be necessary to trace these original forms in order to do a complete analysis and account of the language. Socrates was on the right track!

The *Cratylus* is an intriguing work by Plato and became the foundation for future arguments about the nature and origin of language. In the play, Cratylus is the character who argues tenaciously that the names for things are naturally correct. That there is a natural and fundamental relation between a thing and the name for it. Cratylus continues by insisting that knowledge of things is the same as knowledge of names and "lying" is impossible. Socrates plays devil's advocate by maintaining that "naming" is a special art and responsive to human desires. Socrates points to the great variation in languages and asks how the differences could have come about. But Cratylus is unimpressed and insists that these differences are due to unimportant differences in societies and these have nothing to do with the truth function of language. Socrates skewers Cratylus by asking: If knowledge of things is through names, how could the first name giver have known anything? Cratylus resorts to the same answer given by many before him and after. He claims that the first names for things were given by a power greater than ours.

The *Cratylus* was important because it posed a question worth asking at the time. It marked the first time that the conventional nature of language was treated as a serious possibility. Interestingly, Aristotle reports later that Cratylus grew old and became convinced of the naturalness of change and abandoned the use of language altogether. When asked a question, he would only point to things.

Throughout the centuries, many scholars speculated about the relationship between language and people. The question about how language originated became so frustrating that some academic organizations banned its discussion. Nevertheless, as we move toward the modern time, the study of language was assumed to be a natural evolutionary process and not a gift from God. In 1755, Kant explained that language was the result of gradual evolution and natural causes that influenced the development of humans. Charles Darwin, in *The Descent of Man*, showed that all animals (humans included) had some form of communication system and that the distinctions among them were of degree and emphasis. Humans, of course, can create more precise articulation and distinct meaning than say, a dog, but the dog that recognizes his owner is employing some rudimentary symbolic capabilities. Darwin made the wise and important distinction between the essential biological impulse of language and the varieties of symbolic behavior. It is important not to forget that language has a fundamental biological basis.

Language and Biology

Humans are part of the animal world, so language and communication are biologically based. The human mental ability to use language and process information, including our articulatory mechanisms, results from the unique biological evolution of humans. We are the only animals that speak with such specificity and sophistication. Although humans have unique linguistic and communication capabilities, all organisms "signal" one another in some way. A rather classic article by Hockett (1960) outlined the best way to classify and compare all communication systems. He termed these *design features* and explained how all animals communicate using these design features to varying degrees. The 13 design features are described briefly and Table 1.1 illustrates a sample comparison among species.

1. *Vocal-auditory*. Language is speech. It is produced by the mouth and received by the ear. The vocal-auditory channel means that the sender and receiver have a vocal tract for producing sounds and an auditory mechanism to receive sounds.

2. *Broadcast transmission and directional reception*. This means that a signal travels in all directions. When I speak, anyone within earshot can hear me. The sounds of my voice are not narrowly beamed in a single direction. You have seen this at work if you have ever been overheard by someone whom you did not intend to receive the message.

TABLE 1.1
Hockett Design Features and Comparison Among Species

Feature	Human Language	Bee Dance	Gibbon Calls	Paralinguistics
1. Vocal-auditory	Yes	No	Yes	Yes
2. Broadcast transmission	Yes	Yes	Yes	Yes
3. Rapid fading	Yes	?	Yes	Yes
4. Interchangeability	Yes	Limited	Yes	Yes
5. Total feedback	Yes	?	Yes	Mostly yes
6. Specialization	Yes	?	Yes	Yes
7. Semanticity	Yes	Yes	Yes	Yes?
8. Arbitrariness	Yes	No	Yes	Yes?
9. Discreteness	Yes	No	Yes	In part
10. Displacement	Yes	Yes	Yes	Mostly no
11. Productivity	Yes	Yes	No	Yes
12. Traditional transmission	Yes	Probably no	?	Yes
13. Duality patterning	Yes	No	No	No

Note. Adapted from Hockett, 1960, and Akmajian et al., 1980.

3. *Rapid fading.* The sound of your voice goes away quickly. As soon as I utter something, the sound dissipates in a matter of milliseconds.

4. *Interchangeability.* A member of the species with this feature can be both sender and receiver. Mechanical communication devices sometimes do not have this communication feature; they are either senders or receivers.

5. *Total feedback.* Senders can monitor their own signals. I can hear myself speak and respond in some way.

6. *Specialization.* The communication system serves no other function; it is specialized.

7. *Semanticity.* Expressions have meaning. Sounds or words in human language can have many meanings. They relate to ideas and information in the world. The chirping of a bird is part of the bird's signaling system but it has very limited meaning.

8. *Arbitrariness.* The signals do not have a natural connection between themselves and what they stand for. Any sound could be used to stand for the word *house*. The fact that there are so many languages and different words for the same thing is a good example of arbitrariness.

9. *Discreteness.* This refers to the fact that signals are unique and discrete. There are many elements in the communication system that can be organized in different ways for communication purposes. For example, the words *tin* and *fin* are distinguished by their initial sounds. Human language is digital in that its basic elements (sounds) can be separated and recombined.

10. *Displacement.* When messages do not have to be in the context that produces them they are displaced. A human can talk about something in the past, present, or future, in a real or imaginary world.

11. *Productivity.* Communication systems that are creative and allow for an unlimited supply of messages are productive.

12. *Traditional transmission.* Human language is learned anew by each generation. It is taught to children and not genetically programmed. The ability to learn a language, but not a specific language or communication, is genetic.

13. *Duality of patterning.* The communication system has two independent subsystems, one of sounds and the other of meanings and interpretations. The sound system is physical, and different combinations of sounds make for an infinite set of messages.

Table 1.1 shows a comparison across species for each of the design features. For example, bees do not communicate using a vocal-auditory system as do gibbons, humans, and aspects of paralinguistic communication. You will notice that humans use all of the design features. They have much in common with other species, but the differences are the result of biological differences among the various species. Humans, for example, have larger portions of their brains devoted to information processing and smaller portions devoted to motor and physiological needs. In Fig. 1.1, you can see that rats have a larger portion of their brain devoted to olfactory senses. So smell is much more important to their evolutionary adaptation and functioning. The brain of lower animals is almost wholly taken up with sensory and motor functions. Primate brains (humans and chimps) are larger and have more brain space that is not necessary for basic functioning and is available for higher order linguistic and cognitive ability. Thus, humans do not have the best eyesight or sense of smell, because these are less important to survival, but they are capable of sophisticated thought processes.

Human language is very productive. We have many terms and ways to organize them to produce an infinite corpus of speech, writing, ideas, and

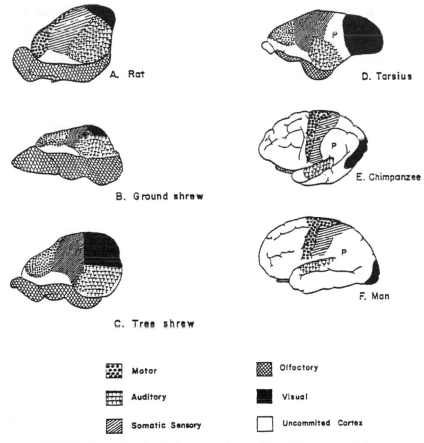

FIG. 1.1. Mammalian brains from rat to human. The white areas, called association cortex, represent tissue not committed to basic brain functions. This area is dramatically increased in humans. Reprinted with permission from Penfield (1966).

so forth. The bee dance is also considered productive by Hockett's (1960) system because bees can produce many dances to give many directions as to where to locate food. But Hockett's system fails to capture some important differences and complexities. Bees can produce many dances but only about one thing—the source of food. There is no meaningful way to define the limits of human language use. Human language is not only productive but creative. Humans have the same biological imperative as other species; that is, we must feed ourselves, protect ourselves, and reproduce. But humans can transcend instinct because of our linguistic and cognitive abilities. Humans are as much a product of culture and mind as of nature.

The Rise of Language Study

If it were possible to identify a single year that marked the beginning of contemporary linguistic science, it is the year 1786. This is the year that Sir William Jones of the East India Company presented his famous paper establishing beyond a doubt that classical Indian Sanskrit was related to Greek, Latin, and Germanic languages. This work formed the first stage in the systematic growth of historical and comparative linguistics. The Italian merchant Filippo Sassetti reported similarities between Italian and Sanskrit as early as the 16th century. The word "snake," for example, was *serpe* in Italian and *sarpa* in Sanskrit; seven was *sette* in Italian and *sapta* in Sanskrit; god was *dio* in Italian and *deva* in Sanskrit. But it was Jones who wrote the often quoted paragraph that asserted:

> The Sanskrit language, whatever be its antiquity, is of a wonderful structure; more perfect than the Greek, more copious than the Latin, and more exquisitely refined than either, yet bearing to both of them a stronger affinity, both in roots of verbs and in the forms of grammar, than could possibly have been produced by accident; so strong indeed, that no philologer could examine them all three, without believing them to have sprung from some common source, which, perhaps, no longer exists. (cited in Robbins, 1967, p. 134)

The study of comparative linguistics was a turning point in the history of linguistics as a science because the scholarship increased in both sophistication and systematization. Much of the earlier work was fragmented and isolated. The new science of language was stimulated by the Indo-European hypothesis that predicted correspondences between European languages and those of India and Persia. There was the new science of *comparative grammar*, and it was meant to be analogous to *comparative anatomy*. Biologists in the 18th century had met with success by going beyond simple descriptive classification into comparisons of more central dynamics of an organism. Comparative linguists became more interested in the inner structure of a language and how a particular feature of a language functioned in terms of the whole. There was a transition from philology to linguistics, and languages were studied to determine their own structure and place in historical development. Many thought the methods of comparative linguistics would result in the discovery of the original language. But even in the face of tremendous successes reconstructing the history of extant languages, the goal of discovering the origin of language was unreachable.

Jakob Grimm, and his brother Wilhelm, were not only compilers of fairytales but the first to apply linguistic analyses to German folklore and tales. They were influenced by Rask's discovery of sound shifts and stated what is known as Grimm's law. Grimm built on the techniques of comparative phonetics and posited laws of sound change in various languages. The chart in Table 1.2 reproduces the methods used by Grimm and the comparativists. As words were added to the list, it was possible to note the differences and similarities. Grimm noted, for example, that "father" was similar in Sanskrit, Latin, and Greek but that the initial consonant had changed from a /p/ to an /f/. The same thing was true for "fish" and "foot." A /p/ is an /f/ in the Germanic languages, but no such initial consonant change was found for sounds such as /m/ in "mother." After much detailed work and exhaustive data, it is possible to posit a law such as /p/ > /f/, or voiceless stops become voiceless fricatives. This means that sounds that did not use vocal cord vibrations and had an abrupt stoppage of air became sounds that did not use vocal cord vibration and created a vibrating sound by forcing the air stream through a small closure, thereby creating friction. These changes were presumed to have taken place sometime during the first millennium B.C. when the Germanic tribes split from Roman and Greek tribes and other descendants of Indo-European languages. There are many more sound changes that are part of Grimm's law and the law worked perfectly in most cases.

Many scholars were now beginning to seriously question the utility of searching for an original language, a protolanguage. The successes of the comparativists led to increased attacks on earlier thinkers who were often so preoccupied with the mystical or natural origins of language that they posited outlandish theories. Serious linguists were doing comparative phonology or morphology; speculations about the origins of language were left to clergy-

TABLE 1.2
Word Comparisons in Languages

English	Sanskrit	Latin	Greek	German	Old Eng
foot	pada	pedis	podos	fuss	fot
mother	matar	mater	mitir	mutter	modor
father	pitar	pater	patir	vater	faeder
fish	piska	piscis	ikhthis	fisch	fisc

men, amateur ethnologists, and professors of philosophy. Muller's whimsical terminology for the various theories of language origin is still popular today. He termed the onomatopoeic or imitative theories the "bow-wow theory"; those who assumed that language originated in expressive or emotive sounds were considered adherents of the "pooh-pooh theory"; some suggested that linguistic beginnings emerged from the natural vibrating resonance of voices. They subscribed to the "ding-dong theory"; and one author, who was obviously influenced by Darwin, wrote that just as humans developed from a primeval mass of gelatinous matter, so too did language. This was the "jelly-fish theory." Speculation about the origins of language had ended.

LANGUAGE AND HUMAN NATURE

It is easy enough to understand humans as biological entities. What I mean is that we are in a very real way composed and physiologically governed by chemical and physical properties. Much of early philosophy was devoted to discovering a human "essence" or "nature"; that is, a universal substance or truth about human beings that was thought to be at our definitional core. Scientists and philosophers assumed that this nature was "substantial." In other words, a crucial substance or inherent principle that constituted our essence, an innate instinct or faculty that could be empirically observed and amounted to our most outstanding characteristic. When such an essence could not be observed or agreed upon, it was presupposed. Platonic categories and idea types are examples of such presuppositions. The strongest case could be made for human intelligence. It seemed so obvious that humans were intellectually superior to other species that it simply had to be true that we were biologically and psychologically exclusive.

The question remains whether or not there is a useful and defensible way to understand humans that does not rely on biological or psychological essences, or on historical investigations alone. Perhaps it is best to understand humankind from a cultural perspective. We should not diminish the important biological differences between humans and other species, especially with respect to the evolution of the brain, but for the most part, we will accept Darwin as having solved the problem of anatomical and evolutionary differences between species. If there is anything about humans that we want to claim for exclusivity, it is our symbol-using capacity and the influence of culture on symbolic behavior. This is certainly not a new or innovative position. Such an argument is most completely and elegantly stated in Cassirer (1944). "The philosophy of symbolic forms," wrote Cassirer, "starts from the presupposition that, if there is any definition of the nature or 'essence' of man, this definition can only be understood as a functional one, not a substantial one" (pp. 67–68). This means that the essential structures and categories of human nature are born out of the practical requirements of culture. Our nature is existential, and there lies the essence. Cassirer continued: "Man's outstanding characteristic, his distinguishing mark, is not his metaphysical or physical nature—but his work" (p. 68).

Human culture is a collection of activities that culminate in art, language, and science and determine humanity. An understanding of humans requires an understanding of human activity. A true science of humanity is an examination of the common threads that weave cultural activities into a coherent fabric, and these threads are functional rather than substantial. Chomsky (1975) wrote that "language was the mirror of the mind," and the best way to understand fundamental human structures was to understand language. The important feature of Chomsky's work was his concern for the creative and generative process of language rather than the end result of language. And this must be the focal point of a perspective on human culture, language, and communication. For the products of art, language, and communication are surely less interesting and fundamental than the search and ultimate verification of the principles that *generate* these products. We must begin with the assumption that human culture is driven by functional prerequisites and that language, or symbolic form, is the fundamental requirement for culture.

Language and Practical Function

All language is representative. It does not describe or refer to anything directly, but rather it represents various aspects of reality. Even the most concrete reality relies on the representational nature of language. The word "table" is not a table but a metaphoric reference to an object that serves some practical function we typically ascribe to "tableness." It seems logical that if the world must be described in this metaphoric entity called language, then pragmatics must be the primary nature of this entity. Language functions to refer and characterize the world. Moreover, although the capacity for language is biologically determined, an individual's particular language and how it serves him or her is socially determined. A child learning language is mapping the external world onto his or her own mental one. Many individual and cultural differences emerge from this mapping process. It is no accident that language and myth were two sides of the same coin for the primitive mind because the external world of nature and society were so bonded. This is also true of the child's world. The relation between the linguistic system and the world it represents was so intimate that primitive man could not tell the difference between language and what it was supposed to represent. The "words" were presumed to be equally as powerful as the reality. The result was magic and myth. The primitive mind could not tell the difference between language and the external world. But, interestingly enough, magic and myth have something fundamental in common with contemporary science: reality. Early magic and myth was an attempt to describe and understand reality in much the same way that modern social science does. Magic is concerned with causal relations and how one event leads to another, and it is language that is responsible for these relations. Language and myth are real in the same way: ceremonies, rituals, secret words, and incantations are the stuff of the mythical world. We talk about people who are "possessed" and "transformed" by supernatural influences that travel in language. In short, the first functions of language were an attempt to harness and control the world's difficult ways. Language was psychological nutriment. But soon the limitations of language became apparent and magic gave way to semantics.

At some point in the dawn of Greek society, language lost its immediate and transmundane powers. It could no longer solve problems and summon the supernatural quite as easily as once believed. But language remained important. One difference was that language itself became the object of study. Philosophers began to examine the meaning of meaning and how language worked. Language was an important dimension of human existence, but it no longer was considered transcendental. This point in the history of thinking about language was crucial. First, it was the beginning of serious inquiry into the nature and function of language and, second, it placed language at the center of knowledge and truth.

When the Sophists maintained that language was practical, rhetoric—the first theory of communication—was born. The spoken word was very important in Greek society. It is probably difficult for contemporary man to fully realize just how important and potent the spoken word was to citizens of Greece. Sillars (1964) showed how rhetoric was an "act" with all the emotional, legal, and practical realities that the word implies. Skilled use of the language was valuable to a Greek citizen and he was responsible for the consequences of his words. Schools of rhetoric were designed to teach people how to be effective with words; how to speak and act in the world. Rhetoric was part of a theory of knowledge that discounted the objective and supposed natural relation between language and the world. We were still a long way from truly understanding language but, interestingly enough, theories of rhetoric were the beginning.

Language as Social Process

Sociolinguistics is the appropriate contemporary term for the issues and problems that face language and a social community. Although the term has become over-associated with dialects and regional variations of language, it should be used in accordance with its original definition, which referred to any correlation between language use and the social occasion that prompted it. This would include face-to-face encounters, speech acts, speech episodes, and the like.

A *speech community* is at the core of sociolinguistics and has attracted much attention, but its sense remains ambiguous. The concept of speech community is fundamental because it establishes the unit of understanding as social rather than linguistic. One begins with the problems of a social unit (e.g., family, decision-making group, couple, organization) and then considers the entire communication system that constitutes the social unit. Language problems are defined as problems of communication and social functioning. Some theorists, such as Bloomfield (1933), used the term to refer to people who use the same speech signals and thereby emphasize large-scale groups who share a language. Some linguists have used the term in this way to describe the ideal speaker in the ideal speech community. They are concerned with identifying a language and discovering the universal features of that language. The term is used in this case to outline a group of speakers who share a tongue. A second use of the term *speech community* draws on a sociological or anthropological perspective in which a "group of people" is defined according to any of the various cultural or social conditions that occasion their organization.

But language is more than a social group's mechanism for making meaning. Language, or symbol-using ability, is the defining characteristic of humans. Much philosophical inquiry has been devoted to a definition of humankind and I do not attempt to extend those ideas here. However if, as I argue, language was born to serve communication and is, therefore, a social process, some continued understanding of language is necessary.

10 IDEAS ABOUT LANGUAGE

I conclude this chapter with 10 ideas about language that are accepted by all language theorists. These 10 ideas are precursors of all the ideas in the ensuing chapters. I have added the first idea (that all language is fundamentally communicative) but beyond that, these nine ideas come from Harvey Daniels's (1983) book *Famous Last Words: The American Language Crisis Reconsidered.* They are presented in very abbreviated form because later chapters develop them in more detail.

1. *Language is fundamentally communicative.* Communication—the formulation, storage, and expression of meaning—is the only reason for language. Some representational system is necessary for communication; that is, there must be something (e.g., smells, images, chemical reactions, or sounds) that "stands for" or represents reality. For humans, this representational system is composed of sounds that stand for meanings. These sounds, for humans, are more than calls

and cries but form a complex, multilevel code that is more than a simple matching of sounds to meanings. The complexity of human sounds results from the fact that language can have multiple meanings and confused meanings, carries emotional implications, and changes over time.

2. *Children learn language easily and without explicit instruction.* If language were biologically based, as we saw earlier in this chapter, wouldn't it make sense for nature to make it easy to acquire language? Children acquire language as naturally as they learn to walk because our brains are prewired for language. But a child must still live in a language-stimulus environment. A baby isolated at birth would never learn language. Still, parents do not "teach" language; they do not explain language to children. The family communication environment provides a context that stimulates language learning in a child.

3. *Language is rule governed.* When you learn language, you learn a vast system of rules. These rules are mostly subconscious, and you do not need to understand them to use them. There are rules of sounds, words, the arrangement of words, and the social aspects of speaking. The rules are quite arbitrary. Words can change meanings, and rules of sentence structure are different in different languages. In English, for example, adjectives appear before the noun they modify (*dining room*). In Hebrew, the syntax is reversed (*cheder ochel;* room of eating), and in some languages any order is permissible. These differences are no better or worse than one another, they are simply the rule variations that make up different languages.

4. *All languages have sounds, vocabulary, and syntax.* These are the important components of any language, and they are taken up in more detail in the next chapter. The sound system is the inventory of human noises that become meaningful. These meaningful sounds are organized into vocabulary. This vocabulary is developed to represent ideas, things, and actions in the world. Syntax is the organization of words into sentences to represent relations among ideas. All of these components, combined with the practical rules of language use, constitute a grammar, which is everything we know about the workings of a language.

5. *Everyone speaks a dialect.* A dialect is a variety or a variation on the rules of sounds, words, and syntax described earlier. In chapter 8, we see that there are many dialects. There is a tendency to think that some people speak "correctly," that they speak the "right" way. The truth is that everyone speaks a language influenced by their geography, family background, education, and individual experiences. If Southerners say "where y'all goin?" they are not making a mistake;

they are simply using the rules of language learned in their families and region of the country. True, there is what we call a *standard* language that is taught in the schools and used in the official organizations of a culture. This makes for a mutually intelligible version of a culture's language, and it receives a special status as such. But this standard dialect is not inherently superior. It may confer status on its users, but there is nothing that makes it naturally better than any other dialect.

6. *Languages have numerous styles, subdialects, colloquialisms, and slang.* Language is further influenced by individuals, relationships, contexts (e.g., work, home, play), and moods. The variations of our language are even more complex than dialects. We adjust our language to many things. I might use an intimate code when speaking to my wife ("honey," "snookums"), an intimacy that can only occur in close personal relationships. At work, I will be more formal, where my speaking will sound like written language, a language that is more constructed and planned. I will use occupational jargon at work. My language will vary again in a casual context with friends. Individuals control a range of styles and jargons, and one's skill and competence at communication is enhanced to the extent that they have conscious understanding and control of these things.

7. *Language change is normal.* The English language that you speak sounds very little like the English language 500 years ago. All languages change over time. Some sounds become more pronounced and others fall away. The word "knee" is spelled with a *k* because the /kuh/ sound used to be part of how the word was said. Language change is very dependent on politics and changes in cultures. When one group of people conquers another, this produces changes in both languages but more so for the defeated than for the victors. Simplification is one rule of language change. This is why people say *goin* for *going.* As business, industry, and media progress, we have many new and changing vocabulary words. The words "hard drive," "word processing," and "mouse" result from technological advances and the computer industry. The terms serve obvious needs and respond to changes in society. Some words change functions: They began as nouns and have become verbs. The word *memo* used to refer only to a written note (a noun), but it is possible now to hear people say, "Would you *memo* me on that," making the word function as a verb. By the way, the word *memo* came into being as a clip from the word *memorandum.*

8. *Languages are intimately tied to societies and individuals.* All languages are shaped by the people and cultures that use them. Lan-

guage is a very practical device. It is very useful because it is adaptable to many needs. So although all languages share the rules and principles we are discussing, it is also true that they have many particular differences among them. The English spoken by African Americans in many of the urban communities of the United States reflects the experiences of African Americans. As a White person, I would have little success if I tried to speak this dialect. There is a sense in which I have no "right" to speak it. A philosopher once said that "Language is the house of being." He meant that we are conditioned by the language we speak, and it teaches us how to look at the world. We understand the world and develop our sense of reality through language.

9. *Judgments about languages and dialects are a matter of taste.* It is simply impossible to conclude that one language or dialect is superior to another. French is not superior to Spanish, nor English to Swahili, nor a British dialect to a New Jersey dialect, and any judgments about a language or dialect are a matter of individual preference. We have all sorts of images of languages and dialects: German is supposed to be martial and harsh; French is the language of love; British English is refined and intelligent; New York dialects are crude; Southern speakers are slow and dumb. None of these are necessarily true about the languages or the people who use them. We may come to believe them through people we know or media images, but each of these dialects and languages is a fully formed ruled-governed variation that is responsive to its speakers. However, I do not deny that how one speaks influences social acceptability and economic success in America. It is just that this results from social discriminatory processes and not from any intrinsic inferiority of a language or dialect.

10. *Writing is derived from speech.* There are societies that do not write, that have no written forms of their language. But there is no such thing as a society of people who do not speak. Writing is a derivative form of speaking. It is based on a set of visual conventions (alphabet) that represent the sounds of speech. Actually, writing is the first form of communication technology. It requires equipment such as a stylus (pen or a stick) and something to mark (paper or mud). Like speech, writing is subject to many rules and variations. Its conventions of spelling and syntax change over time; it varies along a continuum from highly formal to casual; it is subject to stylistic differences; we make judgments about its quality; and writing has influenced how modern humans think. As the first communication technology, writing is implicated in the communication revolution we are currently experiencing. The development of writing, beginning only about 5,000 years ago, was the first baby step on the journey to computers, databases, and massive information dissemination.

CHAPTER TWO

Modern Linguistics

One of the creators of modern linguistics is Ferdinand de Saussure (1959), who was a Swiss linguist. Saussure is credited with creating a way to look at language that goes right to the heart of the nature of language. Around the turn of the century, when Saussure was working, most language study was of the nature discussed in the previous chapter. That is, it was the tradition of historical linguists. Historical linguistics was preoccupied with studying the origins of language and tracing current languages back to their historical roots.

Saussure did not say much about culture, but he indirectly influenced future work on the nature of language such that culture became more important. Many historical linguists before the 20th century thought that some languages were simply superior. Latin and Greek were considered almost perfect: They were thought to be the language of the refined and educated classes. Until around the 1960s, many high school students were required to take Latin because it supposedly improved the mind. But historical linguists reconstructed the language family tree. The examples in Table 1.2 in chapter 1 illustrate how historical linguists found that languages had more in common than not.

It turned out that our understanding of the superiority of Greek and Latin was more complicated. The evidence showed that the line from classical Greek and Latin to Europe was not so straight, that people in other lands using such languages as Sanskrit had to be factored in. The list of vocabulary items in Table 1.2 is a "structural" arrangement that shows similarities and differences among languages. We can see, for example, that German and English look more alike than other branches of the language tree. True scholarship-oriented historical linguistics is more complicated and takes other factors into account, but the conclusion is the same: A language is a warehouse of vocabulary and grammar, which are sources of comparison to other languages.

Saussure internalized the principles and methods of historical linguistics, but he did not care much about their conclusions. It simply did not matter to him that a word was related to an ancient language in India. But he did care about people communicating. Saussure was interested in how people marshaled a collection of sounds into words—which constituted a symbol system—that were used to communicate. He used a chessboard example that has been repeated many times since: Language is like a game of chess. There are different pieces that do different things and a set of rules about how to play the game. What the chessboard looks like when you begin the game (start a conversation) is different than an hour later. How the game began influences the state of the board later in the game. In communication, like chess, there are strategies for how to accomplish goals and generally get what you want. Saussure made many distinctions and established op-positional categories. At this point, we must introduce some jargon.

Saussure was responsible for three key distinctions in the study of language. First, he posited the distinction between historical linguistics and the state of a language at any point in time. He was determined to define the boundaries of language study. To this end, he began by distinguishing between historical linguistics and descriptive linguistics, or diachronic and synchronic analyses, respectively. *Diachronic* linguistics is the study of language history and change. This was the type of work that characterized most of Saussure's predecessors, because the crucial question about language, at least until the 19th century, revolved around discovering the origin of language. Moreover, scholars believed that the "truths" of language lay in the earlier tongues that were closer to protolanguages. *Synchronic* linguistics, on the other hand, is descriptive linguistics and concerned with the state of a language at any point in time, especially the present. This distinction is significant because syn-chronic analyses were either ignored or overlooked in the past. But most important, the distinction drew attention to the current structural properties of language as well as historical dimensions. A language system is complete and operates as a logical system at any point in time regardless of influences from the past. A language has an existence separate from its history. The language is constituted at any point in time by the people who speak it and, of course, these people are typically ignorant of its history. This may seem like a relatively insignificant distinction, but it served to direct attention away from historical studies and toward contemporary issues in linguistics such as psycholinguis-tics, semiotics, and communication.

This led to Saussure's second contribution: the distinction between *langue* and *parole*. Language is such a complex and varied phenomenon that it would be impossible to study it with any scientific rigor without assuming some basic operating principles. Moreover, it is the ability to produce language and the distinct ideas and meanings of people that are most characteristic of human nature. Vocalization is simply the instrument for actualizing the world of the mind. *Langue*, then, is an abstract system that all of us have in common and enables us to speak. It is the cognitive apparatus that members of a community share that allows them to use a vocabulary, grammar, and phonology to actualize speech. *Parole* is the actualization of *langue*. It is the way we actually speak—the vocabulary, accent, and syntactic forms. The chess analogy continues: The game is constituted by a system of rules and conventions that exist beyond actual games played. There are an infinite number of possible games of chess that can be played, and these are generated by the set of rules and conventions. So it is with language: There are untold numbers of accents, words, syntactical forms (i.e., languages and dialects in the world), and they are all manifestations of *langue* or a set of rules.

A third contribution of Saussure completes his tenets of structuralism. He showed that the principles of *langue* must be described synchronically as a system of elements composed of lexical, grammatical, and phonological components. Linguistic terms were to be defined relative to each other. In other words, an element of the linguistic system is meaningful only in relation to other elements. So the difference between the /p/ sound in *pin* and the /t/ sound in *tin* is established by contrasting articulatory responses necessary to produce the sounds. Moreover, it is this difference that accounts for the difference in meaning between the two words. The difference in meaning between the two words is accounted for by the structural relation between the two initial sounds. The English language recognizes this difference.

This structural-contrast perspective on language and meaning is a radical departure from historical traditions. According to Fries (1964, p. 64), it meant the abandonment of a "word-centered" thinking about language for a "relational" or "structural" view of language. Language was now assumed to be a conventional system of symbols that had an arbitrary relation to reality. The notion that a word had a natural relation with what it stood for was no longer taken very seriously. It was now clear that what made a word "meaningful" was not its particular individual elements, but the *difference* between these elements and others. "Dad" is differentiated in sound from "bad" and "mad," for example; it is conceptually different from "mom," "son," "cousin," and so on. The most immediate and significant impact of Saussure's structural theory was in the area of phonology. It led to the concept of the *phoneme* as a distinct and indivisible sound of a language. It is the speaker's perception of the differences between the initial consonants in "dad" and "bad" that poses a meaningful contrast and allows us to hear and understand the two words as different. The concept of the phoneme is now a linguistic universal.

SIGN RELATIONSHIPS

The science of signs is certainly one of the most significant and exciting contributions of Saussure. He called this science *semiology*, and the developments in this science have been extensive in the past decades.

Saussure described signs as a relation between "concept" and "sound"; to use Saussure's words—*signified* and *signifier*. The linguistic sign is constituted by the structural relation between a concept (e.g., "house"—the *signified*) and the sound of the word "house" (*signifier*). A language is essentially composed of such relations, and the study of language is the study of the system of signs that express ideas. As we discovered before, the relation between sound and concept is arbitrary. The word "house" has no necessary and natural links to the concept of house or to actual "houseness." The noun "house" refers to a structure where people live because the language makes it mean that, and the meaning of the word "house" can only be confirmed within the language. Language, then, is a shaper of the world and a conservative one at that, because we are forced to apprehend the world through the structures of language. "Language," said Saussure (1959), "is a system of interdependent terms in which the value of each term results solely from the simultaneous presence of the others" (p. 114).

Two types of structural relations in a language system presented by Saussure are syntagmatic and associative. *Syntagmatic* relations of a word are those relations that can obtain with neighboring words in a sentence. For example, there is a syntagmatic relation between the words "Roger" and "threw" such that the words can appear in the sentence "Roger threw the ball." This is true of any two words where one performs a subject function and the other a verb function. This is not true for two proper nouns such as "Roger Don" or two verbs as in "thrown threw." If a word changes its relation to a neighboring word, then it changes its identity. So if there were a person whose name was "Thrown," then a particular sequence of sounds that results in the sound of "Thrown" would be a different word. The sentence "Thrown threw the ball to me" would be perfectly sensible. The meaning of the sentence is unfolded as you read along and is not complete until you finish the sentence. *Associative* relations pertain to the ways in which words can replace one another and the ways in which they do not. Part of the meaning of a sentence such as "Bob's wife threw a plate at Bill" is derived by what words and sounds were *not* chosen. We know it is a "plate" and not a "skate" or a "date," and throwing a plate "at" someone is, of course, different than throwing a plate "to" someone. These relations are about how words and sounds are associated with each other and form part of the synchronic relation within the language structure.

The influence Saussure had on language was revolutionary. His work had a profound influence on many aspects of linguistics, but synchronic analysis is one of the most radical because it turned language on itself. He argued that language was a closed and self-defining system, and his work caused linguists and scholars of language to look inward toward the internal mechanisms of language rather than outward to an empirical world. Language was structure, not function; it was form, not substance. The rewards of structuralism are significant. His theorizing led to the generative syntax of Chomsky (1957). And his semiotics or "science of signs" made great headway in understanding verbal and nonverbal modes of communication: Images, musical sounds, rituals, and social conventions all constitute fascinating systems of meaning. But human communication is concerned with function, not structure; its essence lies in use, not form. In many ways, Saussure's work and the work of those who followed directed attention *away* from human communication. The role of language in the history of communication in the past decades is almost absent. We develop this argument more fully later, but for now we can see that Saussure was the intellectual spark for relegating language to the realm of internal logic and structural mechanisms that had little concern for language in context, or how people actually use language to accomplish social goals.

THE LANGUAGE OF LINGUISTICS

Linguistics is the scientific and rigorous study of the formal nature of language. To that end, the study of linguistics has provided us with a vocabulary for talking about language. This vocabulary has been specified and has become widely accepted in the 20th century. It is important that scholars and laymen alike be comfortable with this vocabulary and use it in a consistent manner. Any area of expertise is composed of a basic vocabulary and terms that must be mastered. A skilled auto mechanic has mastered words that refer to the basic parts of the internal combustion engine (e.g., "distributor," "intake valve," "head gasket") and understands how these parts work together (e.g., "the fuel system," "carburetion"). Part of becoming knowledgeable in any field of endeavor (law, medicine, science, communication) is learning the vocabulary of that field. The terms and concepts given here are the building blocks of the study of language and are indispensable for understanding language. We refer to the concepts described here many times throughout this book. In some cases (e.g., discourse), we devote entire chapters to the subject matter. We consider the vocabulary of linguistics in hierarchical order from the smallest unit of linguistic analysis to the largest.

Phonology

When linguists speak of language, they are talking about *spoken* language. Spoken language is essentially a sound system. The phoneme is the fundamental theoretical component of the sound system. One branch of phonetics is called *acoustical phonetics* and is primarily concerned with the physical properties of sounds. This aspect of sounds can be measured by sophisticated technological instruments. One could measure movement in the upper respiratory tract, vibrations of the vocal cords, force of the aspiration of breath from the lungs, muscle movements in the oral cavity, sound duration, tonal composition and intensity, and a variety of other physical properties of sound production and hearing. On the whole, however, linguists have ignored the physical parameters of speaking and listening and have argued that the really important facts of sound systems are something other than such observations can produce. Phonemes cannot be measured but are the theoretical standard by which minimal units of sound can be measured against one another. Linguists are interested in sounds that result in a difference in meaning; that is, sounds as phonemes rather than sounds as breath groups or respiratory movements.

There are about 40 phonemes in English (depending on an individual's accent), but there are a great variety of ways that individual phonemes can be expressed. It is an oversimplification to say that a phoneme is a minimal sound unit, because the pronunciation of a particular phoneme can vary. The phoneme /p/, for example, is pronounced differently in "pity" than it is in "sport." In the first case, you can feel what is called *aspiration,* or a slight puff of air following the /p/. What is important is that this distinction (aspirated, not aspirated) is not used in English to distinguish between the meaning of two words. This is not true of the Thai language. In Thai, these two *p*'s are separate phonemes because they distinguish between word meanings. A phoneme is a mental construct. When we say that the first sound in "pity" is the phoneme /p/, we are making a claim about how the minds of speakers of English work.

Linguists are mostly interested in how sounds are articulated, and this branch of linguistics is known as *articulatory phonetics.* The articulation of sounds is described by the events that occur in the throat, mouth, and nose. One event is the vibration of the vocal cords. When they are vibrating, the sound is called *voiced.* The *b* in "bet" is voiced where the *p* in "pin" is not. Another way to describe sounds is whether or not air exits partially or fully through the nose. If it does, the sound is called *nasal;* if it does not, the sound is *oral.* So the *N* in "Nancy" is nasal, but all of the sounds in "pat" are oral because no air exits through the nose. A third event during sound production is whether or not the flow of air is interrupted. Interrupted sounds are *consonants* and noninterrupted sounds are *vowels.* The type of interruption is yet another issue: The *t* in "tip" is pronounced by abruptly stopping the air, and this type of interruption is called a *stop.* The *f* sound in "fish" is called a *fricative* because the interruption is of a frictional nature.

In the preceding paragraph, we talked about the manner in which sounds are articulated. There are other manners of articulation, but sounds are also classified according to the place of articulation in the oral cavity. The *p* sound in "pin" is produced by placing the two lips together. This is called *bilabial*. The *t* in "tip" is produced by placing the tip of the tongue underneath the ridge above the top row of the teeth. This is called the *alveolar* ridge. The *p* in "pin," then, is articulated by putting the two lips together and abruptly stopping the flow of air. By stating the place of articulation (bilabial) and the manner of articulation (stop), we have identified what is called a *bilabial stop*. The *t* in "tip" is an *alveolar stop*. The *f* in "fish" is pronounced by placing the top row of teeth behind the bottom lip. This is the *labiodental* position so the *f* sound is called a labiodental fricative. The *s* sound in "sip" is an alveolar fricative.

Phoneticians can make fine distinctions between sounds and the various parts of the vocal apparatus used to make sounds. Most people do not hear the slight differences in sounds that result from the location of a sound within the sound sequence of a word. What precedes and follows a particular sound is called the *sound environment*. These environments influence the articulation of particular sounds. The *p* in "peace" is aspirated because it is in the initial sound position in the word. If you put your hand in front of your mouth, you can feel a puff of air after making the sound. But the *p* in "speech" is in a medial position and is not aspirated. This aspiration is one factor that contributes to the differences in accents. If you practice pronouncing the initial *p* without aspirating it, you will be approximating a French accent. Variations on phones are called *allophones*. A phoneme is not a single sound but a family of sounds with slight differences among them. The *i* in "milk" can be pronounced in the front of the mouth or in the back of the mouth and produce a slightly different expression of the same phoneme. These variations are called *allophones*.

It should be clear by now that what are phonemes in some languages are not present in others. In some languages, the manner of articulation creates a different phoneme and different meanings. Nasalization has phonemic value in some American Indian languages. In Towa, the nasalized *kwi* means "wind" but the nonnasalized *kwi* means "a light." In Chinese, the unaspirated *To* means "many" and the aspirated *t'o* means "to take off." Tonality also has phonemic value in Chinese, and this is what gives Chinese its singsong quality. The various tone patterns create different meaning.

It is almost impossible to distinguish phonemes in normal speech patterns. Although phonemic theory and principles of articulation are invaluable for describing and classifying sounds, they do not capture the essence of "real" speech. During actual speech, the vocal organs are constantly moving and do not stop such that one could isolate phonemes. The sounds flow together and form a continuum that is sometimes difficult to decipher. Beginners in a new language usually think that the native speakers are speaking too fast for precisely this reason. The sign sold in joke shops that reads "kwicherbellyakin" is a humorous (I suppose) attempt to capitalize on this fact. All this underscores the theoretical nature of phonemes. When we say the middle sound in "pin" is the phoneme /I/, we are making a statement about a family of sounds in the minds of English speakers.

It is also important to understand the differences between spelling (orthography) and sounds. There is not a one-to-one correspondence between spelling and sounds, and that is why the International Phonetic Alphabet (IPA) was developed. When we spell, it is possible for the same letters to represent different sounds such as the *th* in *th*in versus *th*en, or the *t* in *t*oe compared to the second *t* in sta*t*ion; or different letters can stand for the same sound such as *J*oe and bri*dge*. Although the IPA has been modified over the years to accommodate new sounds, it is a useful notation system for representing the variety of actual sounds that are present in normal speech. One reason for the discrepancy between spelling and speech is that spoken language changes faster than writing. Writing is a conservative influence on a language and changes at a slower rate than speaking. Grammar books and precise rules for writing and spelling are relatively recent in the history of language. When languages were first being written down, there was more correspondence between how people actually spoke and how words were spelled. But as time passes, old sounds drop out of the language and new ones enter. Moreover, people begin to speak differently on the basis of geography, education, work, and so forth, and spelling rules cannot keep up with phonetic changes. In Chaucer's day, the *gh* in "light" and "night" was pronounced; in time, the sound of these words changed but the spelling did not. Men such as Benjamin Franklin, Noah Webster, and George Bernard Shaw have all advocated spelling reform, but change is very slow. Spelling phonetically would certainly be easier for school children and foreigners learning English, but it would probably be impossible for spelling rules to keep up with sound changes. More important, if we did spell phonetically, whose pronunciation would we use? When someone from New York City says "idear" for "idea" should we spell it with the added *r*? Should we spell the word "four" the way someone from Brooklyn pronounces it—"foa"? Needless to say, there probably will not be much pressure to spell phonetically in the near future.

Suprasegmentals. Natural language is digital in that it can be decomposed into discrete units. These discrete sound units are called *segmentals*. As we have seen, it is possible to decompose words into sound segments or segmental phonemes. In addition to these structural properties, there are other oral characteristics that signal meaning during speech. These are called *suprasegmentals* because they are vocal qualities that are superimposed over a string of phonetical segments. These qualities are juncture, pitch, and stress and are quite central to communication, even though most structural linguists pay little attention to suprasegmentals.

Juncture is the slight pause between elements—syllables, words, sentences—and can apply to the time spent articulating a sound (the length of the sound) or the amount of vocal pause between segments of an utterance. The differences between the two utterances below are subtle but distinct:

It's a nice house.

It's an ice house.

Juncture is indicated in writing by commas, periods, and punctuation in general. Punctuation is a sort of stage direction about how to group words and where to pause. The spacing between words in writing is also a visual expression of juncture. But in spoken language, we listen for meaning, not mechanics. So if I mean to ask, "Where did you go?" and I utter it as "Wherja go?" I am able to eliminate the pauses between the first three words because I expect my listener to understand the meaning of the utterance.

Pitch results from the vibration of the vocal cords. The pitch is higher when the vocal cords are vibrating more rapidly. Pitch frequency results in a change of tone which, as we have seen, is very important in some languages. But unlike Chinese, pitch in an individual English word does not affect its meaning. The word "book" has the same meaning whether it is pronounced in a high, medium, or low pitch. How a listener is to interpret the function of an utterance is also determined by pitch. If the final syllables in "He asked Mary" are a falling low pitch, the utterance is a statement. A high rising pitch would cause the utterance to be heard as a question: "He asked Mary?"

The final suprasegmental is *stress*, or loudness or softness of an utterance. It is the amount of intensity given the vowel of a syllable. Stress can affect the meaning of a word or a sentence but it is mostly responsible for noun–verb contrasts in English. The word "permit," for example, with the accent on the first vowel (e) is a noun. It is a thing you have. If the stress is on the second vowel (I), the word is a verb: "I will not permit it." The same is true for words like "contract" (noun) and "contract" (verb) or "subject" (noun) and "subject" (verb). Some languages are called *fixed stress languages* because they do not shift stress from vowel to vowel. In French, the stress is always on the last syllable; Polish always stresses the penultimate or next to last syllable. English, Spanish, Russian, and others are free stress languages, where the stress can shift from syllable to syllable and significantly affect the meaning of a word.

Morphology

It is possible to consider the basic building blocks of language to be hierarchically arranged. Phonemes are the smallest units of sound, and when they are strung together they make *morphemes*, or the smallest group of sounds that have meaning. A morpheme is a meaning unit. The word "house" is a morpheme because as a noun, it is an indivisible meaning unit that refers to a structure where we live; or, when it is a verb, the word refers to the act of providing accommodations for someone. But if we were to add an "s" to the word "house" and make it "houses," we would change the meaning of the word, albeit slightly. Anytime a sound functions as a grammatical unit to influence the meaning of a word, it too is a morpheme. So the "s" added to "house" is also a morpheme because it makes the word plural and makes the word mean "more than one house."

A word like "house" or "dog" is called a *free morpheme* because it can occur in isolation and cannot be divided into smaller meaning units. The "s" that was added above is called a *bound morpheme* because it must be attached to another meaning unit. The word "quickest," for example, is composed of two morphemes, one bound and one free. The word "quick" is the free morpheme and carries the basic meaning of the word. The "est" makes the word a superlative and is a bound morpheme because it cannot stand alone and be meaningful. The morpheme that comprises the essential meaning of a word is called the *base*; the bound morpheme that attaches to the base is called an *affix*.

Linguistics recognizes two classes of bound morphemes. The first class is called *inflectional morphemes* and their influence on a base word is predictable. Inflectional morphemes modify the grammatical class of words by signaling a change in number, person, gender, tense, and so on, but they do not shift the base word into another form class. When "house" becomes "houses," it is still a noun even though you have added the plural morpheme "s." These inflections actually make our language easier to use. In English, anytime you want to make something plural you simply add the plural morpheme "s." There are some irregular forms (e.g., man:men or child:children) but for the most part, it is easy to form the plural in English. This consistency in inflections makes forming the comparative and superlative easy also. The "er" morpheme compares one thing to another, and the "est" morpheme is the superlative. I can say "Bob is quick," "Jim is quicker," and "Mary is quickest."

Derivational morphemes constitute the second class of morphemes and they modify a word according to its lexical and grammatical class. They result in more profound changes on base words. The word "style" is a noun, but if I make it "stylish," then it is an adjective. In English, derivational morphemes include suffixes (e.g., "ish," "ous," "er," "ly," "ate," and "able") and prefixes (e.g., "un," "im," "re," and "ex"). Some derivational morphemes do not radically change the meaning of a base word. Adding the "er" morpheme to make a noun an agentive noun (the person who does something) does not radically alter the base word. Someone who "runs" is a "runner" and someone who "throws" is a "thrower." All words that end in "er" are not composed of the "er" morpheme. Words like "anger," "butcher," and "mother" utilize the same phonetic ending to the word, but these are not agentive noun morphemes. A mother does not "moth"! These odd cases are often confusing to the foreigner or second language learner.

Just as there are phonetic variations called allophones, there are morphemic variations called *allomorphs*. These are typically phonetic variations within a morphological class. The most common example of this is the plural morpheme "s." When writing a plural word, we simply add the letter "s." But pronouncing a plural depends on the phonetic environment. The "s" sound in "cats" is an /s/ because it follows a voiceless stop. But the "s" sound in "kids" is a /z/ (kidz) because it follows a voiced stop. The plural of "bushes" is an /iz/ sound. These are all the plural morpheme but pronounced differently. Other allomorphs are irregular plurals, such as "oxen" as the plural of "ox" and "children" as the plural of "child." Finally, there are what are called *zero classes*, where the singular and plural forms of a word are identical. The plural of "sheep" is "sheep" and "deer" is "deer."

Some languages are highly inflected. Latin is perhaps the most highly inflected language. In Latin, an inflectional affix is used to grammatically modify a word to signal a change in gender, person, number, and so on. Following is a comparison of Latin to English.

porto	I carry
portas	you carry
portat	he, she, it carries
portabo	I will carry

It is easy enough to see that although Latin is highly inflected, English is less so. English depends much more on separate auxiliary elements, especially pronouns.

Morphological Classification of Languages. Finally, the languages of the world have been classified according to morphological similarities. Some languages, such as Chinese, have isolated morphemes for each lexical item. These languages are called *analytic* because they can be broken down into individual morphological units. Analytic languages are composed of morphemes with separate meaning or grammatical standing. The morphemes do not affix to one another. English is also quite analytic but not nearly as much as Chinese. For the English sentence "This is my house," the Chinese version would be translated literally as "This + is + I + possessive + house." The English pronoun "my" is a possessive pronoun in that it indicates person and possession. In Chinese, the fact that the house was owned by the speaker would be communicated with a separate word (morpheme). *Syn-*

thetic languages are at the other end of the continuum from analytical ones. Synthetic languages are highly inflected, such as Latin, English, French, Spanish, and German. But extremely synthetic languages are called *polysynthetic*, because instead of separate morphemes in a sentence with a few inflections, polysynthetic languages begin with one base morpheme and affix morphemes to it until it becomes the entire sentence. This category was created for American Indian and Eskimo languages. The following is the Eskimo word for "house" and an example of how this base word can be developed into variations.

igdlo	a house
igdlorssuaq	a large house
igdluliorpoq	he builds a house
igdlorssualiorpoq	he builds a large house

The final morphological classification is *agglutinative* and is most descriptive of non-Indo-European languages such as Turkish and Japanese. Agglutinative languages are similar to inflected languages, but there is more regularity in the affixes and bases. Agglutinative languages have morphemes that have attached to roots and become fused with them. The important differences between agglutinative languages and inflected languages is the stability of the roots. In English, we say "to love" and in Turkish it would be "sev-mek"; "to be loved" would be "sev-il-mek" in Turkish. The English word "love" becomes "loved," but the Turkish roots remain constant.

Some earlier theorists (e.g., Jesperson, 1922) who speculated about the origins of language on the basis of morphological structure suggested that language is changing in a reasonably consistent manner. They proposed that human language developed through three stages, beginning with analytic languages that were irregular and happenstance. There was one morphemic utterance (usually a simple syllable) representing one idea or concept and no logical or grammatical harmony. From here, some roots attached to others (agglutinated) and lost their independence so as to be fused with the other root and form a logical relation. The third stage was flexional such that grammatical information (tense, plurality, etc.) became coded into the root.

Jespersen (1922) maintained that a "law of development" is possible. Jespersen asserted that evolution of language was from inseparable irregular conglomerations to freely and regularly combinable short elements. Even vocabulary, according to Jespersen, develops in a manner parallel to grammar. He stated that advanced cultures have more information, especially abstract information, coded into a word. The Zulus can talk about a "red cow" or a "white cow" but no word for the general concept "cow." Much has been made of the languages of various peoples of the world, but it is always difficult to generalize. The languages of primitive tribes are not necessarily simpler than the language of more technologically advanced cultures. Detailed study of these languages reveals the intricacies and complications of the grammar and usage. Words are functional, and if a culture develops separate words for different numbers of the same class of objects, this simply reflects the importance of these different groups. Languages do reflect the reality of a culture, and although it is tempting to assume that some languages and cultures are inherently better than others, it is typically an error to make such an assumption.

Syntax and Grammar

Ordered arrangements of phonemes make morphemes. Strings of morphemes make sentences, and sentences are the concern of syntax. *Syntax* is that aspect of grammar that is devoted to the order or arrangement of words in a sentence. The sentence "The ashtray is ugly" is composed of sounds—morphemes—and these are ordered according to rules of sentences. A sentence, in the formal sense, is really a unit of discourse in written communication. We do not really speak in sentences; we speak in word groups and phrases with numerous beginnings and endings, but they are not neat and orderly sentences. The structure of a sentence, however, is related to the structure of natural (oral) human communication, because all sentences are composed of subjects and predicates, and this is little more than a grammatical coding of the fact that any utterance is structurally composed of a topic and a comment on that topic. Grammar has become associated with syntax because its popular usage refers to "correctness" of language use such as subject–verb agreement. Technically, a *grammar* is a set of principles governing a body of knowledge and often concerned with the rules that guide sequential ordering. There is such a thing as a grammar of mathematics or a grammar of music. In linguistics, grammar typically refers to the scientific study of the phonological, morphological, and syntactic structure rules that explain how language works. Grammar does not usually concern itself with meaning (semantics) and rules of communication, but we see later that much of this is changing.

Syntax is especially important in English because word order determines meaning in English. All languages adhere to syntactical rules of one sort or another, but the rigidity of these rules is greater in some languages. It is very important to distinguish between the syntactical rules that govern a language and the rules that a culture imposes on its language. This is the distinction between descriptive grammar and prescriptive grammar. *Descriptive grammars* are essentially scientific theories that attempt to explain how language works. The goal of the descriptivist is to simply state how language actually works. People spoke long before there were linguists around to uncover the rules of speaking. The intent of descriptive grammar is to posit explanations for the facts of language use, and there is no assumption of correctness or appropriateness. *Prescriptive grammars,* on the other hand, are the stuff of high school English teachers. They "prescribe," like medicine for what ails you, how you "ought" to speak. Newspaper columnists and pundits who continually decry the state of the language are arguing for the concept of "correct" usage. If someone asks me how much money I have and I respond with, "I don't have none," I am using a sentence that, according to contemporary teaching, is ungrammatical and is poor usage. From a purely communicative perspective, the sentence is just fine. You would know exactly what I meant if I said "I don't have none." People use constructions such as these all the time. But grammar books caution against using double negatives and say that one should utter "I don't have any." The first sentence is not "wrong," it is prescriptively wrong. A communication theorist who was analyzing how people actually spoke would be quite interested in this usage. He would want to know who used utterances of this type, in what context, and why. The linguist would want to explain the origins of the utterance and how it fits into current theories of grammar.

Prescriptivism is a remnant from the days when Latin was considered the perfect language. Most of the first literate people, that is, people able to read and write, were members of the church, and church documents were written in Latin. An earlier popular grammar book was written by Bishop Robert Loth and he, among others, prescribed how language should be rather than how it actually was. These prescriptive grammarians tried to force-fit English syntactical structure into Latin structure. So because Latin nouns had six cases, English nouns were supposed to have six cases. Rules of Latin were often indiscriminately applied to English. When students are taught not to split infinitives, it is because they cannot be split in Latin. The difficulty is that the rule is logical in Latin because infinitives were one word, and of course one word should not be split. But in English, most functions are indicated by particles, so inserting a word between two words is plausible. It is quite communicative to say that you are going "to diligently inquire . . ." rather than be constrained by a rigid rule that says you must say, "to inquire diligently . . ." It should be acceptable "to consciously split infinitives."

The extent to which syntax contributes to the meaning of a sentence is called *structural meaning.* Lexical meaning is typically within the purview of semanticists and pertains to what words symbolize and their detonations and connotations. We obtain lexical meanings from dictionaries and other resources that document definitions, origins, and common usage. Structural meaning depends on a formal analysis of how words combine. In the sentence "The friend of the mother and the father will arrive soon," it is possible to attach two different meanings to the sentence. One person—the friend of the mother and father—may be arriving; or, two people—the friend of the mother, and also the father—may be arriving soon. The ambiguity in this sentence is called structural ambiguity because it is attributable to more than one way for the word elements to combine into meaning. The sentence would be lexically ambiguous if there were a word that we did not understand.

Function words and inflections are another way that structural devices contribute to the meaning. *Function words* are words that serve grammatical purposes and do not refer to specific objects or ideas in the world. Words such as "but," "and," "the," and "any" are function words. These elements of a sentence have no meaning in isolation but serve to signal the listener to combine or relate groups of words in a particular way. What if I tell a child that he or she can have "cake and ice cream," but I really mean to say "cake or ice cream." The resultant difference in meaning is considerable because "and" instructs the hearer to include both elements on either side of it (cake and ice cream), whereas "or" implies one element but not the other. English is less inflected than a language like Latin, because we use more function words such as articles and prepositions to indicate the case function of the word. In Latin, *homo* means "the man" as the subject of a sentence. In English, we use the definite article "the," indicating a specific man, and its function as the subject of a sentence is dependent on its position in the sentence: "The man (subject) hit the ball." If "the man" is in the object position, the Latin term is *hominem*, but the English equivalent is still "the man": "The ball hit the man (object)." Again, Latin is inflected and builds the function of the term into the word itself, whereas English uses function words such as articles and prepositions and relies on syntactical order.

Syntax, like phonology and morphology, is rule governed. Any sentence can be decomposed and altered by the application of certain rules. Consider the following sentence as an example: "The teacher yelled at the students." The hearer (or reader) of the sentence presumably understands the meaning of the words (teacher, yelled, student) and the way in which the function words direct the relations among the elements of the sentence. But it is also possible to group these words into phrases that make the structure of the sentence more apparent.

The combination of the first two words is called a *noun phrase*. Syntactic rules state that noun phrases can function as subjects or objects of sentences and only noun phrases can do so. "The teacher" is the subject noun phrase and "the student" is the object noun phrase. There is always an adjective slot for use at the speaker's discretion. I can modify the nouns by inserting an adjective into the position preceding the nouns. I could say "The nasty teacher yelled at the poor students." It is permissible to insert any number of adjectives into the adjective position. It would be grammatical for me to say "The big, ugly, weird, strong, strange, intelligent, aggressive, nasty teacher. . . ." Such a construction would be strange and perhaps in poor style, but it is perfectly grammatical. Verb phrases can contain verbs, noun

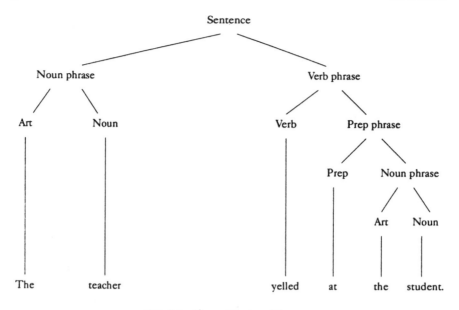

FIG. 2.1. Phrase Structure Diagram.

phrases, and prepositional phrases. Figure 2.1 indicates all the elements beneath the verb phrase.

When people are learning a language, they "understand" these rules and permissible sequences at an unconscious level. Which of the following can legitimately complete the blank?

"The room ————."

a. big class
b. because the application
c. emptied quickly
d. the person

A native speaker "knows," even if only intuitively, that c is permissible because the sentence must contain a verb phrase. Knowledge of these rules is valuable, because they allow you to make sense of sentences that you have never encountered before. You do not learn a language by memorizing sentences that are allowed. You learn a few rules and apply them in an infinite number of cases. Your knowledge of structural rules is central to the production and interpretation of sentences, and the example below is a rather dramatic illustration of this point. What if you encounter the following sentence: "The sluddish porgath boffed opily in the gert."

If you were asked to identify the subject of the sentence, you would have little trouble naming the "porgath" as the subject of the sentence. Now, what is that porgath like? It is sluddish. What is the porgath doing? Boffing. How is it doing it? Opily. Where is it doing it? In the gert. You know these things about the sentence because the sentence satisfies certain syntactical rules (and phonological ones). The sentence is grammatically correct but semantic nonsense.

Most contemporary linguists are more concerned with the rules that account for the string of words in the sentence than with the semantics of the sentence. Applying meaning to the sentence, according to many linguists, is simply a matter of establishing references to the empirical world for each word. The lexicon (vocabulary) is often considered the simplest part of a grammar. Assume we had the following dictionary definitions for the words used previously (eliminating the function words):

sluddish *adj.* Slow, not moving quickly.

porgath *n.* A bear-like animal having a long snout and shaggy hair.

boffed *v.* To swim or move through water.

opily *adv.* To be happy or do something in a happy state.

gert *n.* A shallow body of water.

The sentence would be about a slow bear-like animal that was swimming happily in some body of water. But many linguists assume a structuralist perspective where word order and formation rules for sentences are considered the basis of the grammar of a language. Words and their definitions and etiologies usually play a very small role in the world of the professional linguist. The contemporary linguist has been accused of concentrating on structure and ignoring meaning. The accusation is somewhat exaggerated but not completely.

Linguistics and Communication

The scholarly tradition of linguistics is only marginally concerned with communication. The term *communication* appears in much linguistic literature but usually as a way to refer to the general function of language and not as an object of study unto itself. In fact, traditional linguistic inquiry is driven by a set of assumptions that removes communication from consideration. But language is a group as well as an individual possession. Communication is its primary function even though the tradition of linguistics ignores communication. The major emphasis has been on assuming language to be an autonomous system and explicating its formal characteristics. But communication has been ignored for another more simple reason: Communication is complex and more difficult to study than phonology or morphology. Communication is more dependent on meaning, context, and individual cognitive and perceptual apparatus than anything else. We must certainly understand the formalities of linguists but they are less pertinent to communication than a number of other principles and theories. Consider the following sentence: "I like my apple."

We have seen all the linguistic issues one could bring to bear on this sentence. But things get a little more difficult when we enter the realm of meaning and communication. The "communicative" function of this sentence is difficult to analyze. An "apple" could refer to a fruit or a make of computer. Although any theory of semantics can account fairly easily for the two references for "apple," the semantics of the verb "to like" are more difficult. What does it mean "to like"? And how about all of the different ways that the same word can be used? In some ways, these questions pertain to cognitive processing and are treated in chapter 3. But what are the other effects and consequences of this utterance? What if the person who spoke just before the utterance said, "My IBM computer is the best made" and you followed with "I like my Apple." How does the utterance *function*? What is its meaning? Would you then be having what we call a *disagreement*? What if these are the words of a salesman and a potential customer? Then they function and mean something a little different. Speakers learn sounds and grammatical forms to be sure, but they also must learn how to use language in different circumstances. Communication is essentially a matter of situated language use. The remainder of this book is devoted to understanding the principles and forms of communication; or, how language is used in situations.

CHAPTER THREE

Language and Cognition: Comprehending Messages

The mind is the bridge that connects the body to the soul; it should be possible for the mind to explain the relation between genetics, cell structures, and so forth, and the roles and problems of men and women in society. But it cannot do it very well. The realms of physiology and culture are incommensurate and rely on different vocabularies. It is as if we were trying to build an explanatory link between the sound of a drill on a construction crew and the music of Mozart; it cannot be done.

But there is one vocabulary that just might help us with this connection. It is the domain of symbols, their systems and products. Symbols like words or icons, symbol systems like language or math, and the outcomes of symbol systems like theories and explanations allow us to traffic in the realms of "noise" and "music"; symbol systems can provide at least some links between biology and culture. This is true because all knowledge must be cast in a symbol system of some sort. Biology and literature may be quite different, but both must be understood, and in some senses are constituted, in accordance with a symbol system. Our ability to symbolize is a major fact of our human nature. Other species in the animal kingdom cannot do it. Although we do not "will" things into existence, we can only know them through symbols. Inanimate objects such as rocks and trees exist separate from our knowledge of them and have functions and processes of their own, but as soon as we approach an object and label it or try to understand something about it, we must rely on symbols. Even the act of labeling an object (e.g., "rock" or "tree") establishes a symbolic relation because the label is not the thing itself, and the label influences our understanding of the object. This is especially true for objects or ideas that do not have clear

referents; labels such as truth, beauty, justice, and freedom do not refer to the empirical world, so their ability to define the nature of something is even more powerful.

All acts of cognition are symbolic. A child is born capable of performing certain biological functions such as sucking, crying, and so on, but the child is also biologically prepared to think and symbolize. At first, a newborn will suck anything because the response is instinctual, but very soon the child "knows" what to suck and what to avoid because he or she has categorized those objects that are pleasurable and productive and those that are not. This categorization is the child's first experience with meaning and rudimentary cognition. Humans must interact—that is, communicate—with the world. We are in one instance born alone as a sophisticated problem-solving machine, and in another, a product of a culture that we must "experience" and shape ourselves to conform to.

The perspective held by Noam Chomsky (1975) is the one most in accord with a view of humans as problem-solving machines. Chomsky assumed that the environment plays a limited role in the development and performance of human skills. Language development in children is, according to Chomsky, a matter of triggering predetermined principles. The mind is anything but a *tabula rasa*; rather, it is composed of a set of laws and rules that will lay dormant unless triggered by environmental stimuli, but such laws and rules are not created or fashioned by the environment. Chomsky's perspective has been useful in many ways because it serves as an important adjustment to empirical accounts of cognitive development. It seems unreasonable to assume that fundamental cognitive skills are *learned* in the traditional learning theory sense of the term.

But Chomsky's arguments do not recognize the importance of symbolic capacities and the fact that human mental abilities are awash in meanings and interpretations that vary across cultures. Other theorists such as Scribner and Cole (1981), and most notably Geertz (1972), worked in direct opposition to Chomsky by maintaining the primacy of culture. These scholars maintained that the forms and powers of culture are responsible for individual development. They denied the mentalism of generations ago, which assumed that individual capabilities were biologically determined, and the claims of theorists like Chomsky who assign a very minor role to culture. These culturalists stress the extent to which cultural symbols and collective wisdom are responsible for ideas and ways of thinking (e.g., Shotter, 1993). Rather than assuming that humans are an autonomous calculating device, culturalists propose that the systems of meaning and interpretation in cultures influence these core intellectual apparatus and are essentially responsible for their nature. Theorists such as Geertz assume that the mind is a cultural achievement. An individual's cognitive powers are absorbed from outside him- or herself.

LANGUAGE AND MIND

It is possible to forge a path somewhere between innate intelligence and claims for the primacy of culture. There is a position that assumes the centrality of innate human intellectual abilities and the extent to which these are influenced by cultural practices. Such a position is "symbolist" in nature. It relies on the writings and theories of people like Cassirer (1953–1957) and Susan Langer (1942) and distinguishes humans from other organisms by their ability to use symbolic vehicles to express and communicate meanings. Language is the fundamental symbolic vehicle of all cultures, and it alone is both an integral part of our biological storehouse of intelligences and the cultural structures that form our ideas and ways of behaving. In my view, along with David Olson (1970), Howard Gardner (1985), and others, it is the deployment of various symbol systems that accounts for our distinctive human nature. Any of us may be skilled at math, language, music, or visual arts, but all of these are symbol systems that operate according to intellectual principles and are, of course, culturally specific. The more specific relation between mind and natural language is of concern to communication. Although there are other systems of symbolization, natural language is the most fundamental. It pervades mental life but does not constitute the whole of mental life. We possess emotions, feelings, and cognitions that are not language-like. But here we examine models of language and cognition and take up issues in language and mind as they relate to communication. In his provocative book *Frames of Mind* (1985), Howard Gardner discussed other symbol systems or intelligences such as musical intelligence, spatial intelligence, and bodily kinesthetic intelligence, and he concluded that people vary with respect to skills in these areas. But linguistic intelligence is the heart of mental life.

In recent years, there has been a continuing debate that pits "behaviorists" against "mentalists." A generation ago, there was no such debate because most scholars assumed a behaviorist position that language learning was essentially a complex stimulus–response system learned like any other habit. B. F. Skinner (1957), in his book *Verbal Behavior*, wrote that conclusions derived from laboratory work on rats were sufficient to describe human language behavior. John Watson, the father of American behaviorism, assumed that thought and speech were the same thing; he wrote that thought processes were directly related to motor habits in the larynx (Watson & Raynor, 1920). The eminent Soviet psychologist L. S. Vygotsky took a less extreme position. Vygotsky (1965) argued that language and thought are very close in a child when he or she is learning to think and speak. When a child thinks, he or she speaks. But as the human organism develops, it is no longer constrained by external stimuli, and thought and speech become more separate. After about the age of 6, the inner mental life of a human being becomes more autonomous. Piaget (1950) offered related arguments—and was clearly opposed to the behaviorists—by suggesting that cognitive development precedes linguistic development. He concluded that the mind interacts with the environment and gives rise to the linguistic process. Piaget's work has been very influential in convincing a generation of thinkers to take a whole view of the child and his or her development rather than adopting a structuralist position that fragments the ingredients of language and cognitive abilities.

Up to now, we have been using the terms *language* and *speech* a bit sloppily, and it is important to make some distinctions. The early behaviorist position is really quite easily discarded, because they failed to recognize the differences between language and speech. *Speech* is a physical process. It is concerned with the physiological production of sounds and is quite easily measurable and observable. *Language* is an abstract system of meaning and structures. A language is composed of symbolic elements that exist on a variety of levels (e.g., phonemes, morphemes) and rules for arranging and using these elements. The behaviorists were talking about speech and thought, not language and thought. The biological processes that govern speech are perhaps related to thought in some interesting manner, but these processes are probably quite separate from the mechanisms that describe language and thought. The cognitivists such as Piaget were essentially interested in language and thought, or the structures that relate inner linguistic processes with cognitive ones. It is certainly easy to demonstrate that physiological speech is not necessary for thinking that relies on linguistic principles.

It is also true that thought is not just inner speech, where inner speech is used to mean a one-to-one mapping between an idea and spoken words. The map that guides us from a thought to a particular verbal expression is surely a complex and poorly understood one; a map with little detail. The same thought can be expressed with many words. If I wanted a friend to open a door, I could say it in any number of ways using a variety of words and sentence structures. I do not "think" the request in an analytic manner where I imagine each separate word and action. Thoughts seem to be present all at once and then sent elsewhere for processing, where they are packaged and made suitable for expressions in speech. Language is only one system of representation. Artists, scientists, and mathematicians all report that their insights come in many forms and often do not even resemble language. But language is the system of representation that concerns us here, and even though there are other interesting and provocative symbol systems, we must now turn our attention to specific issues in language processing and representation.

PSYCHOLINGUISTICS

The term *psycholinguistics* refers to the psychological principles involved in how language is processed and represented. Before 1957, psychologists were not very interested in language in the same way as linguists. Psychologists assumed that language was some sort of complex word association established through reinforcement, the position essentially espoused by B. F. Skinner (1957) in *Verbal Behavior*. Most psychologists were not very familiar with particular issues in linguistics, and their attempts to develop suitable theories about psychology and language—psycholinguistic theory—rested on an inadequate description of language in general. But in 1957, Chomsky published *Syntactic Structures* and radically changed the direction of linguistic work: New issues came to the foreground and old ones receded into the background.

Insufficient generality and theoretical depth was one of the consequences of early theories of language. Early theories assumed that language could be modeled as a process with probabilistic functions that describe the left-to-right movement of a sentence as in the following sentence: "The man who works in the building eats here often." Analysis of this sentence would assume that "man" follows "the" with some probability and according to a linguistic principle connecting definite articles to nouns. The same is assumed to be true of all other words in the sentence, but we run into difficulties when we encounter "eats" following "building." Buildings do not eat and these words are unrelated because "eats" refers to "man" in this sentence, and "man" is six words back. Because embeddings in sentences are unlimited, a left-to-right surface structure cannot fully describe sentences. Chomsky (1957), in fact, showed that it was impossible.

Another problem with early linguistics was that it had trouble with ambiguous sentences such as "The shooting of the hunters was terrible." The sentence is ambiguous because it could mean that the hunters were poor shots or that it was too bad that hunters were shot. The words have different grammatical functions depending on how you interpret the sentence. There are other problems with linguistics (see Chomsky, 1965, 1966; Lyons, 1969), but they can be reduced for our purposes to a failure to include the role of cognition in language. The structures of grammar were simply too complex to be learned according to the principles of behaviorism. There had to be some form of grammar programmed into the brain.

Chomsky's Linguistics

Noam Chomsky took issue with the behaviorists and adopted a mentalist and rationalist approach to linguistics. The publication of *Syntactic Structures* in 1957 was a remarkable intellectual achievement and produced a revolution in the study of language comparable to Freud's influences on psychology. We cannot take up the full details of Chomsky's work here, but the interested reader is referred to original sources or accounts for newcomers that appear in Langacker (1973), Lyons (1969), and Liles (1971). Moreover, many of the technical and philosophical details of Chomsky's writings are of less concern to us than his influences on psycholinguistics and language processing. In many ways, Chomsky's work is minimally related to principles of communication because he stated rather emphatically that language use—the essence of communication—held little interest for him. We see later and in other chapters that Chomsky relegated communication to linguistic performance and failed to treat it seriously. We also see, however, that Chomsky has been criticized for failing to understand language as fundamentally a communication process (Searle, 1974), and others have tried to adjust his theory to include the semantic and communicative components of language. We delve into Chomskyian principles and contributions only as far as necessary to understand current thinking about the relations between language and mind. Communication is assumed to rely on linguistic processing because human decisions about meaning, the effects of messages, and various communicative skills are dependent on how language is processed.

Sentence Units and Grammar. Bloomfieldian linguistics was a sort of verbal botany. All the little parts and elements of language (e.g., phonemes and morphemes) were classified and organized into different levels. Meanings were assumed to be patterns of stimulus and response and within the realm of psychology. Chomsky found that the methods he had been taught as a student worked well enough with phonemes and morphemes because there was a finite number of them. But the number of *sentences* in a natural human language is infinite. Humans can produce an unlimited number of sentences and any single sentence can be made even longer and modified by adding adjectives. For instance, the following sentence is grammatical: "The little boy who walks home from school every day with his friend went into the store to buy some penny candy for his sister who drives her red sports car home every day."

Such a sentence is grammatical, although it is not one we would likely use because we might lose track of what we were talking about. The addition of an infinite number of adjectives or relative clauses would lengthen the sentence, yet it would remain grammatical. But we do learn to produce and comprehend an infinite number of grammatical sentences. How can this be? We certainly do not learn by memorizing all of the sentences that we use. People utter and comprehend sentences all the time that they have never been exposed to before. It must be that we do not learn sentences themselves but a finite set of rules for producing sentences. Also, as we said before, the surface structure of a sentence is not sufficient for understanding a sentence. Therefore, we must know something about sentences at a deeper and more fundamental level than what we see and hear. It is the relation between this deeper level and the surface level that concerned Chomsky. He changed the goal of linguistics away from the classification of linguistic elements toward creating a theory that accounts for all sentences. The theory would describe which strings of words would be counted as sentences and the structure of these sentences.

The theory should generate sentences such as "Willie was in love with Margaret" but not "Love in Margaret Willie with was." This is the point at which Chomsky becomes significant to psycholinguistics. Chomsky claimed that humans had a "tacit" knowledge of grammatical rules that was biologically grounded. The grammarian's ability to generate these rules was proof that they existed. Chomsky took this assumption to be a rationalist view of linguistic knowledge and associated his work with Descartes and Kant, who believed that certain parts of our cognitive machinery were innate. A child is presumed to be born with a *universal grammar*—a set of principles common to all languages—and this universal grammar is what allows the child to learn language so effortlessly. The child "learns" a particular language, but he or she does this from the foundation of universal grammar. This universal grammar is part of a speaker–hearer's knowledge of language and is called *linguistic competence* by Chomsky. This places linguistics as part of cognitive psychology and in the province of the psycholinguist, whose job it is to describe the processes that access and utilize language. Competence is part of the code for all speaker–hearers, it is part of the mental equipment of the language user. The psycholinguist is in the business of describing this mental reality that is responsible for actual language learning.

Linguistic performance, on the other hand, refers to actual language behavior in concrete situations. It is concerned with the actual languages that people speak and all of the situational and psychological influences that come to bear on members of a speech community. The actual words, sentence structures, slips of the tongue, false starts, and so on that characterize everyday language behavior is the province of linguistic performance. Chomsky's distinction between competence and performance is important because it is a distinction between the mental knowledge necessary for language and a theory about implementing that knowledge. Overt language use (communication) reflects how language is processed and understood and results in theories that produce idealized versions of the processes that determine language behavior. Chomsky argued that in order to understand language performance, it was necessary to understand the structure that generates performance along with other necessary psychological faculties such as memory, attention, recall, and so on.

Chomsky therefore returned linguistics to the realm of psychology, something that Bloomfield worked so hard to avoid. Chomsky's work stimulated a tremendous amount of research and model building regarding the cognitive processes necessary for language processing. Much of the current work in artificial intelligence, teaching computers to think and make decisions, can be traced to Chomsky's earlier theorizing about the competence–performance distinction. The competence–performance distinction has also been roundly criticized (Kaufer, 1979; Searle, 1974; Sutherland, 1966) and we take up some of these criticisms in a later chapter. But first, it is important to fill out Chomsky's theoretical position and to examine some of the models and thinking about language processing.

Linguistic Universals. Conceiving the mind as a predetermined entity that influences the structure of language is a logical consequence of Chomsky's position, especially the principle of linguistic competence. The argument is that this innate mental structure is uniquely human. It follows, therefore, that all human language should have a common form. One goal of the psycholinguist is to explain a language in such a way as to show that language is a logically produced variant of the universal structure. This allows for knowledge claims across languages rather than just within them. Some of the universals are phonological, syntactic, and semantic units. All languages, for example, have grammatical classes such as nouns and verbs and sentence structures that can be classified as having a subject and a predicate. It is also possible to identify articulatory and acoustic properties of sounds that are universal. The fact that children of all languages go through the same phasic development during language acquisition has been used as an example of universal structures that direct the nature of language. At best, language universals are generally plausible, but they have yet to be identified and stated in a particular way.

Transformational Generative Grammar. Transformational generative grammar is a key component of the Chomskyian system and another logical consequence of Chomsky's arguments and philosophical assumptions. Transformational generative grammar is a detailed and precise theory and the reader is referred to Chomsky's original work or Searle (1974) for the most complete explanations.

If there are innate structures that direct the form of language, then the goal of the linguist is to state the phonological, syntactic, and semantic rules that describe this knowledge that a person has. The grammar is *generative* because it must be capable of producing an infinite number of sentences even though only a few sentences are actualized in a particular situation. The sentence that I have just written or a particular one that I uttered in class the other day are sentences that I have never produced before, and more than likely, the reader or hearers have never encountered those exact sentences, but they are still grammatical and understandable. Chomsky's grammar must be generative because the theory requires that it be possible for a few rules to "generate" an infinite variety of sentences for situations. A second use of the term *generative* by Chomsky pertains to the necessity for rules that produce sentences without conscious thought. Sentences must be produced automatically and mechanically.

The grammar is *transformational* because it includes certain types of rules that perform transformations. These rules operate with logical precision, but the principle behind the rules is really quite simple and necessary for the theory. The core of the theory makes it necessary for a few rules to create an infinite number of sentences. These rules exist to perform transformations on *deep structure* and produce surface structures (actual sentences). Deep structure is part of the innate knowledge of the language user and is common across all languages. Surface structures are what differentiates individual languages. Consider the following sentence: "Karen, who is a good cook, made the pasta dinner."

The sentence is derived from a deep structure. We can use our intuitions to see that the sentence can be analyzed as being composed of what are called a matrix sentence and embedded sentences. The matrix sentence is the elemental proposition of the sentence and corresponds roughly to an affirmative declarative sentence.

Matrix sentence: Karen made the dinner.
Embedded sentence: Karen is a good cook.
Embedded sentence: The dinner is pasta.

We can parse the sentence into phrase structures and conceptualize the sentence as diagrammed in Fig. 3.1. These sentences are represented in deep structure and must be "transformed" into the surface structures or sentences that we commonly employ. The transformation rules allow us to make alterations so that we can represent deep structure in surface structure.

Notice that the embedded sentences are influenced by the matrix sentence. We need the transformation rules to delete and rearrange various aspects of the embedded sentences so they will be represented in the matrix sentence according to surface structure principles of the language. An example of a transformational rule would be one in which "Karen is a good cook" becomes a relative clause, and "The dinner is pasta" gets transformed into an adjective. An adjectival insertion rule, then, states that if the noun of an embedded sentence is the same as the matrix sentence, it is permissible to delete the noun and move the adjective to the front of the same noun in the matrix sentence. The same basic rule applies to the subject Karen and the fact that she is a good cook. Karen can be deleted in the embedded sentence and replaced with the relative pronoun "who." The argument is that these two transformation rules operate on the deep structure to produce the surface structure sentence "Karen, who is a good cook, made the pasta dinner."

It is important to note that this is a theoretical representation of the knowledge that a speaker should have to produce language in the way that we do. It certainly is not the case that the mind actually goes through this

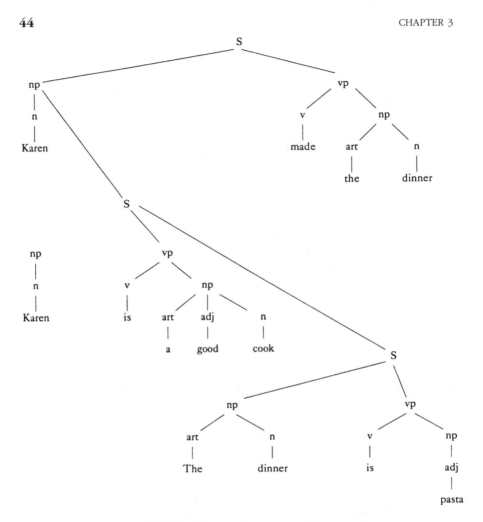

FIG. 3.1. Diagram of sentence relations.

process. The goal of the theorist is to construct a formalism that represents "tacit" knowledge, not consciousness. Chomsky did argue that grammars should reflect what is stored in the mind, but it is unlikely that there are parallels between formalisms and the way the mind works.

Grammar and Psychological Reality. The 1957 version of *Syntactic Structures* focused on syntax more than meaning or sounds. The result was a shift away from meaning and a move toward studying types of transformations. In *Aspects of a Theory of Syntax* (1965), Chomsky specified the deep structure–surface structure distinction and at least addressed the issue of semantics. But his critics suggested that meaning was more central to demonstrating how sentences work than perhaps syntax or at least more important than previously assumed. One line of work began to examine how "real" grammars are, that is, whether or not it was possible to find empirical illustrations of these abstract cognitive models. A number of investigations tried to assess the reality of transformations.

The assumption was that sentences that required few transformations would be easier to recognize or manipulate in some way than sentences that required more transformations. One investigation (Miller & McKean, 1964) measured how long it took participants to match active sentences with passive ones and found that it took longer than to match affirmative sentences to negative ones. So matching "Bill liked the dog" to "The dog was liked by Bill" was slower than to a corresponding negative sentence such as "Bill didn't like the dog." These results were assumed to be supportive of the psychological reality of transformations because passives are regarded as linguistically more complex than negatives. Other studies (Gough, 1965; Slobin, 1966) asked participants to determine the truth value of different sentence types (e.g., passive–negative, active–affirmative, passive, negative) in relation to pictures and various situations. These studies used response time as a measure and found that passives required more time to evaluate than active sentences. Further investigations (Johnson-Laird, 1969) used quantifiers in sentences such as "All philosophers have read some books" and "Some books have been read by all philosophers" and found that participants confused the explanation of the sentences. Even though each sentence is ambiguous in the same way, the first sentence is typically interpreted as "some book or other" and the second sentence as "some books in particular." Findings in experiments such as these caused researchers to alter their grammars, because underlying meaning relations were perhaps accounting for results as much as the proposed theoretical assumptions.

Current work takes a much more skeptical approach to relating grammatical descriptions to mental operations. Few theorists believe that such mental operations will be revealed in a response-oriented task. Psycholinguists are hesitant to directly equate linguistic complexity to mental operations. The term *complexity* is also full of problems. Should complexity be measured by the number of transformations, type of transformation, sentence structures, or semantic relations? Other questions persist, such as the relation between sentence structure and memory, and it is debatable whether syntactic and semantic information are treated alike in memory or by the generative grammar. There are many ambiguous and contradictory results. The mind is the blackest of all black boxes and its inner workings are not very accessible.

Models of the mind and intelligent guesses about how the language system works are interesting and important. But communication specialists are a little more concerned with comprehension; that is, how actual oral or written messages (texts) are processed, how people construct meaning, or how they formulate hunches about meaning and then come to a decision. These approaches work bit by bit to "construct" the meaning of a message and, unlike Chomskyian approaches, they do not look for single generative mechanisms. This next section extends on basic language processing by focusing on the cognitive implications that relate to semantics and discourse. Some of the specifics of these issues continue in chapters 5, 6, and 7. The remainder of this chapter is devoted to the primary mechanisms involved in how people listen to or read texts to understand them.

TEXT PROCESSING

There is a Sherlock Holmes story where Holmes finds a hat at the scene of a crime. Holmes examines the hat and then concludes that the man who owned the hat has recently had a loss of fortune, a haircut, is overweight, and family troubles. Holmes's reasoning was that the hat was once considered expensive and stylish but is now old. A man who could have afforded the hat would have purchased a new one by now. There were cleanly cut hair ends stuck to the lining of the hat, indicative of a recent haircut. There was perspiration moisture indicating sweat, because the man was overweight. The hat was dusty and unkempt, indicating that his wife was no longer around to clean it for him. The reasoning of Sherlock Holmes is not unlike the reasoning you go through every day to determine the meaning of messages. You too are trying to solve a mystery as you read these words or listen to a friend. Holmes uses the hat, and its various features such as age, style, and cleanliness, as indicators. He makes connections between the state of the hat (the indicators) and what those states "mean."

Every time you encounter language use, every time you read something or listen to someone, the language that you read or hear acts as an indicator, giving you directions about possibilities for meaning. I say "possibilities" because for much of the time, you are making "hunches" about meanings and formulating preliminary hypotheses. As you read or hear more of a text, you encounter new information that gets integrated into your older information on the way to a decision about what something means. All of this happens very quickly and without conscious thought on your part. The goal of a communication specialist interested in text processing is to describe the component processes involved and how they are organized and integrated in order to explain how people understand routine communications. There are many issues that must be included here, such as neurological operations, phonetic processing, visual recognition, and sentence processing. We do not include all of these here but focus on the comprehension process and the features of communication that influence it.

There is much work directed at understanding the processes described next (e.g., Badzinski & Gill, 1994; Bower & Cirilo, 1985; van Dijk, 1988), representing various perspectives. The information-processing approach assumes that understanding text is a matter of perception and then going through a series of stages. In general, when you encounter a word, you identify it and its properties, extract its significant features, classify it as an instance of some kind, and then relate it to a pattern of meanings. Theories of how people comprehend represent these processes as a flow of events from one stage to another. We track this flow as it moves through its steps and use an example to illustrate the comprehension process. Assume you hear the following utterance in a conversation or read it in a story.

(1) I lit up my cigar and now I am in the doghouse.

Your task as a comprehender is to identify the function of each word and come to a meaning decision. If you are reading the sentence, you must begin with a recognition of the visual patterns that make up the letters. You must detect the sentence as a stimulus. Your retina will segregate the words and you will identify the features of the letters (lines, angles, intersections). Next, you will try to classify the stimuli. You have stored in your long-term memory (LTM) prototypes of words that you can match against the incoming stimuli. Very simply, you have in LTM an image and meaning for the word "cigar." That image includes the letters of the alphabet that correspond to the written word "cigar." You take the stimulus word "cigar" and match it against your stored prototype. The matching technique looks for visual, auditory, and semantic similarities and makes a fit. How accurately you match depends on many things, including the quality of your stored prototype, the accuracy of your sensory identification, and the number of possible alternatives. Familiar words and sentences are understood more easily and quickly because the match between the familiar stimulus words and your prototype in LTM is facilitated by your expectations.

Short-Term Memory

After you recognize and classify something, you put it in short-term memory (STM). STM is a working part of your brain that holds information and symbols for a short period of time because they are the focus of attention. STM (a) is active in that it is working rather than just a holding place for long-term information, (b) makes for faster access to information, and (c) stores more specific features of the immediate stimuli. For example, if you saw Sentence (1) written, your STM would store and recognize the shape and design of the letters and other more immediate features. LTM only holds the semantic information and would have no need for storing the graphic images of the letters. Finally, (d) STM is very limited. Because it is designed for immediate practical use, it holds less information.

STM holds information that is functionally useful at the time of communication. The word "doghouse" is composed of two words, "dog" and "house," that go together to form a conception of a place where a dog lives and sleeps. But STM holds the concept doghouse as one concept rather than two words. Moreover, STM holds the intended meaning of the term. The utterance is not designed to refer to an actual doghouse but to the implication that someone is unwelcome and in trouble.

Information in STM can be rehearsed and focused on to keep the concept fresh and available in STM. If one focuses sufficiently on the meaning of a word in STM, it will make its way to LTM. If you tell me a phone number to dial, I can hold that number in STM. But if I practice saying the number, memorize it, or associate it with some known patterns (e.g., 123–4567), then the information is transferred to LTM and becomes more stable. It is interesting to note that information is attended to on the basis of the message producer's goals. If I am reading the newspaper with the goal in mind of finding certain information, that increases the likelihood that I will select and identify certain information.

Long-Term Memory (LTM)

LTM is where more permanent information is deposited. It includes all things the individual "knows" and are not currently in use. The ingredients of LTM are many, including symbols, associations, properties of people and objects, spatial relations in the world, and knowledge of language. It is very useful to understand what types of knowledge people have, because this can be used to design messages for maximum effect and information value. Very simply, your LTM has the meanings of the words in our example sentence stored. All the rules for using pronouns (e.g., "I") and conjunctions ("and"), recognizing grammaticality as explained in the previous section on transformational grammar, and particularized meanings (e.g., "cigars are considered smelly" or "the doghouse") are stored in LTM.

LTM also includes information about relations. Statements such as "If someone lights a cigar, then open up a window" are stored in LTM. You have stored a series of typical actions and behaviors. What we often call misunderstandings or miscommunication can be explained in part by differences in LTM storage. If one person has the belief stored in LTM that cigars are disgusting and smelly, and another thinks of them as aromatic and delightful, then certainly confusions and problems can arise.

Perhaps the most important function of LTM is to store what are called *associative networks*. These are networks that carry the individual's set of relations among semantic concepts, all of the various meaning connections

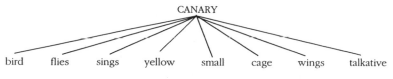

FIG. 3.2. Network of semantic relations stored in LTM.

in your head. You can think of these as networks of associations. If I utter the simple sentence *I have a canary*, the concept "canary" is located within a network of relations. Figure 3.2 is an example. The semantic concept "canary" has all these structured parts and variables that interact with many other concepts. Canaries are known to sing a lot. So we have termed anyone who talks a lot as a "canary," referring to someone who is talkative and reveals information. The simile "he sang like a canary" relies on your knowledge of the semantic network in Fig. 3.2. One's entire history with a word is very important for determining meaning.

Both STM and LTM must be activated. *Activation* is when the links in the semantic network are energized. The utterance or visual presentation of the word "canary" activates the concepts in the network. At some level of activation, the contents of STM or LTM are part of foregrounded consciousness. Information, for example, can move from LTM to STM. Activation spreads along the network and is called *spreading activation*. One link energizes another, and this activation moves along the network. If a speaker says "he sang like a canary" and this is followed by "yeah, and he is yellow too," then calling someone "yellow" is more easily understood because it has been activated by the CANARY concept. All of your concepts and meanings for the term "cigar" are moved from LTM to STM and activated once I utter Sentence (1).

MESSAGE FEATURES OF COMPREHENSION

In chapter 6, we discuss schemas, or broad cognitive structures for representing general concepts. These are the general scripts, images, and assumptions you carry around about how the world works, what goes with what, different roles, and cultural expectations. If I said to you that "Frank was enjoying his brandy and a cigar," you would activate some typical schemes about Frank's identity, his income, age, and so forth, because you hold general cultural schemes about brandy, cigars, and the people who consume them. For now, we must explore the active nature of the meaning process a little more.

Badzinski and Gill (1994) explained how the act of understanding a communicative message is active. That is, people encounter language and build a representation of what it means by combining the language to be understood with already existing background knowledge of the comprehender, along with other resources. This active meaning making is important to understand because it does away with more mechanical notions of meaning. Some early simplistic theories described meaning as moving in a straight line from the source of a message to the receiver, via oral or written language. The source of the message presumably knew exactly what he or she wanted to say and was responsible for putting this into words that traveled to a receiver of the message. It was the job of the receiver to extract the meaning.

In reality, one builds a representation of a text. This is a theoretical estimate of what something means. This is done from a combination of two broad approaches: an approach called "bottom up" and one called "top down." The bottom-up process is the more difficult one. This is where the receiver of a communication encounters text and tries to take the facts of the texts (words, grammatical function) and fit them into a larger framework. Comprehension in this case depends a lot on the quality of the larger framework. If I have a lot of background information about American history and I read a history book, then I have solid interpretive frames for what I read. But if I have no background frames and I am reading history (such as when a young person reads history for the first time), then it is difficult to understand. Perhaps you have noticed that the more you know about something, the easier it is to understand new information. This is because the new information can be integrated somehow into the schema that you already have. Top-down processing is when you use your existing meaning frames to interpret language. Bias, prejudice, and rigid thinking can result when one uses only top-down processing. If you have a set of beliefs and use them in all situations to interpret messages, this leads to highly predictable or rigid interpretations. Almost all comprehension involves some combination of both top-down and bottom-up processes. There are more detailed examples of these in chapters 5 and 6.

Features of Discourse That Influence Comprehension

Discourse features are all the devices and cues that activate a particular representation of a text. In other words, when you are listening to someone speak or reading something, there are features of people, texts, and situations that cue you about how to understand what it is you are hearing or reading. For example, if you are in a conversation with someone you do not know very well and they have an accent such that they pronounce the word "four" as "foah," then that would cue you as to the person's geographic origins. You might conclude that they are "from the east" and then employ any interpretive frames (including stereotypes) you have to understand their message. There are too many discourse features to enumerate here, but Table 3.1 summarizes most of them.

TABLE 3.1
Classifying Discourse Features

Source Features
  Group/ethnic identity: race, gender, socioeconomic status, group affiliation
  History: topic knowledge, relationship with receiver, familiarity with content, knowledge
    of situation
  Personal features: power, warmth, enthusiasm, psychological profile, intelligence
  Disposition: goals, expectations, motivation, arousal, affective state
  Skills: ability to encode message, perspective-taking ability, flexibility, verbal proficiency
Contextual Features
  Physical setting: type of situation, people involved, norms
  Affective climate: mood, tension
Message Features
  Lexical: connectives, diversity of items, repetitions, paraphrases, restatements, coloring
  Syntactic: word order, sentence structure, dialect features, topicalization, sentence length
  Rhetorical: metaphors, humor, irony, question-asking, similes, tropes and figures, puns,
    hyperbole
  Paratextual: headings, bold type, illustrations, punctuations, type size, italics, underlining
  Paraverbal: facial/vocal expression, gestures, smiles, gaze, rate, fluency, intonation/vocali-
    zation patterns, volume, pitch, resonance
Receiver Features
  Group/ethnic identity: race, gender, socioeconomic status, group affiliation
  History: topic knowledge, relationship with source, familiarity with content, knowledge of
    situation
  Personal features: power, warmth, enthusiasm, psychological profile, intelligence
  Disposition: goals, expectations, motivation, arousal, affective state
  Skills: ability to decode message, integrate information, sensitivity to markers, memory
    ability

Note. From Badzinski and Gill (1994). Reprinted by permission.

So, for example, the source of a message may use an accent as described previously or be a member of an ethnic group. The source may have personal features that you admire or not. A speaker or writer has skills such as verbal virtuosity or knowledge of rhetorical strategies. All of these influence in minor or major ways how the receiver of a message makes a decision about meaning. Table 3.1 lists context features, message features, and receiver qualities, all of which trigger a framework or interpretation of a message.

Why are these things important? How can knowledge of these discourse features improve your communication skills? There are three aspects of comprehension that are influenced by skillful use of discourse features. The first is the *nature of inferences* made by the receiver of a message. Discourse features guide inference making. Often there are numerous possible interpretations for messages and the source's use of certain discourse features can assist with the desired meaning. For example, a study by Badzinski (1991) demonstrated a very simple conclusion. In this study, children heard a story about milk that was accidentally spilled. In one case, the story was told in a strong and stern voice, and in another situation, the same story was told in a milder voice. The children made more inferences when they heard the story in a strong voice. Vocal quality cued the children about how to understand the story. An intense voice might cause the children to believe that the storyteller was angry and that spilling the milk was wrong rather than an accident. Moreover, the inferences made varied by age of the children.

Discourse features also influence the likelihood that the receiver of a message will remember certain things. One can increase the recall of a message by manipulating how information is presented. Everyone recalls information that is deemed to be high in importance, even children (Lorch, Bellack, & Augsbach, 1987). Why a receiver of a message considers information important is very complex and influenced potentially by his or her own nature, the source of the message, and the message content itself. But finding ways to cue the receiver that certain information is especially important is a skill practiced by good teachers, writers, politicians, and clergy.

The *speed of processing* is also influenced by discourse features. Sometimes it is important to process information quickly, such as in instructional situations or when listening to someone about something important. Three kinds information is processed quickly, namely, important information, structured information, and familiar information. When you are focusing and listening intently because the information is important, there is a tendency to process the information more quickly. This may be attributable to increased concentration. Information that is highly structured is processed more quickly. Structure is a clear arrangement and organization of the information. A speaker will facilitate speed of comprehension if he or she says something like "I have three points to make tonight" and then very clearly states and describes those points. The listener has been cued by the text and had a certain amount of the cognitive effort done for him. The ideas are arranged and hopefully relate to one another, so the listener has less mental work to do and thereby increases his speed of understanding. Finally, and this seems to be common sense, you process information more quickly when the information is familiar to you. Familiar information activates frameworks of understanding that you already have and thereby increases the speed of comprehension.

Accurate and useful models of how language is processed and how the source of a message can assist the receiver with the burden of interpretation are important. It is the nature of meaning and understanding that it is continually negotiated by integrating incoming information with other sources of knowledge to construct a representation of what a message means. This means that understanding is dynamic and changeable. Knowing how the various parts fit together brings us closer to how communication works. Meaning is the most common goal of language and communication, and the remainder of this book is devoted to various issues in meaning. After considering some technical matters in the concept of meaning, we turn our attention to discourse and message levels of meaning.

CHAPTER FOUR

Meaning

The "meaning of meaning" is probably the single most controversial issue common to linguists, communication theorists, logicians, and psychologists alike. In the previous chapters, we have examined formal issues in language and communication, with an emphasis on the linguistic system and text processing in particular. We come now to the essence of language and communication—the meaning system. Assuming one accepts the obvious fact that the entire nature, structure, and development of language is a vehicle for communication or meaning transmission, then it is certainly odd that linguists, psychologists, and communication theorists have spent little time studying meaning or avoid it altogether. Bloomfield (1933) knew that meaning was the weak point in linguistics, and his successes would have been limited had he concentrated on this problem. Chomsky escaped the problem by assigning syntax to the central role in grammar. This does not detract from his contributions to linguistics and psycholinguistics, but syntax is not meaning and, as Chomsky freely admitted, the "understanding" sense of meaning is far removed from computing syntactic structure.

The Problem of Meaning

People have little or no difficulty working out the meaning of most of what they hear or read, yet the concept of meaning is complex and difficult to explain. The syntactician has worked out models that describe what the human language processor must do to comprehend and produce sentences. The semanticist or meaning theorist must do the same; however, the domain of meaning is more stubborn and intractable than syntax. It does not lend itself to neat logical analyses. Nevertheless, a complete understanding of meaning must account for certain qualities of language. Some of these qualities are listed below.

1. Many words are *associated* with one another. Things would be simple if the world were divided into neat units and there was one word corresponding to one idea or thing. But there are many shades of meaning that are communicated by a set of related words.

   • ghost, spirit, apparition, spook, poltergeist
   • cheat, swindle, fleece, rip off, defraud, deceive

2. Words are *ambiguous*. They can take more than one meaning in a sentence.

   • This plant is tough. ("skin is thick" or "healthy")
   • Don't dribble. ("bounce the ball" or "drop food")

3. Words can be *redundant*. The meaning of one word can be contained in the meaning of another.

   • He killed him dead.
   • We paired them in twos.

4. Poetic uses of language result from the possibility of combining words in some strange ways. One can place *contradictory* and *anomalous* words together to create interesting and new meanings.

   • The sun kissed the forsythia bush. (anomaly)
   • When he stood there was a thunderous silence. (contradictory)

Some semblance of communication occurs because we assume that we have knowledge of the meanings of these words—and how they are formed into sentences—and this knowledge is shared among language users. But knowledge of words and their meaning is not equally distributed in the population and many confusions, distortions, and general breakdowns in communication are attributable to uncoordinated knowledge of word meanings. The ability to understand someone is not the same as the ability to understand the concept and nature of meaning. Although there are a variety of issues involved in understanding "meaning," one distinction is of particular importance: the difference between *reference* and *sense*. A word has a referential quality in that it refers to or stands for something in particular. The referent for a word is typically one thing or idea and represents its core meaning or what the word denotes. The word "Karen" as in "My wife Karen" denotes a specific person. The word "chair" in the phrase "My chair is comfortable" refers to a single empirical object. Any word such as "run," "hit," or "blue" has a set of objects or qualities that it denotes. The *sense* of a word, on the other hand, is related to the practical and common uses of a term. All the possible dictionary entries for a word roughly correspond to all the possible senses of a word. The word "chair" can refer to the object I am sitting on, but I can also say "I am going to chair the meeting." This is a different sense of the word. In the sentence "My son swung at the ball, and his mother, at me," the word "swung" is used in different senses. Both refer to the same essential physical activity, but they have different purposes, motivations, and goals.

There are other "senses" of the word *meaning* that are more applicable to communication issues. When you ask the meaning of a word such as the word "computer" in the sentence "What does the word computer mean?" you are asking about a class of objects and qualities. You would be correct if you said that a computer was a machine that performs calculations of various types. The meaning refers to abstract qualities. But in actual utterances, phrases, or written sentences, words typically refer to specific things. If you asked "Where is my computer?" you would be asking about a specific computer, and the answer would require knowledge of the world or reference to facts that you understand. The interesting distinction is that human communicators are rarely in doubt about the meaning of individual words uttered during actual communication. If I asked someone about the location of my computer, they would know what I meant and would answer in accordance with their knowledge of its whereabouts. But, curiously, if I asked someone for a complete and exhaustive definition of a computer, they would have trouble satisfying my request.

The point here is that words and sentences denote specific things and have a variety of senses about them. A complete theory of meaning must account for both types of meaning. A native speaker computes both types of meaning for a word and, as we learned in chapter 3, a speaker can make educated decisions about the variety of possible senses of a word or phrase. This is called *comprehension*. It is also true that if I ask you about the location of my computer, you might understand my question as an "accusation." There might be a subtle implication that you acquired my computer unlawfully; only our relationship and general knowledge about things would decide whether or not this implication was warranted. A theory of semantics should be capable of accounting for the many senses of words and utterances.

SEMANTICS

Semantics is the study of meaning and probably the most difficult and troublesome aspect of language. It involves many complex issues. Theories of semantics tend to come from two traditions. The first is most closely associated with the field of linguistics and is called *structural semantics*. This is a tradition of technical conventional meaning. In other words, it seeks to explain objective meaning and emphasizes sentences and words that are correct descriptions of the world. Structural semantics does not refer to individuals and their psychological interests. It attempts to cast words and sentences into logical relations that are correct, logical, and true statements. Structural semantics is concerned with conventional meaning. This is the most basic essential meaning—it is literal meaning. Thus, the conventional meaning components of the word "baseball" would include concepts as "round object," "sport," "hard," and "rawhide." But your associations with the word "baseball" that cause you to think of "warm summer afternoons" or "America's pastime" are not part of the word's conventional meaning. These are additional cultural and personal meanings. You might think of the phrase "low fat" as meaning "good for you," but this has nothing to do with the conventional meaning of the two-word combination. Advertisers and artists skillfully manipulate terms that evoke additional meanings.

A second set of issues in the study of meaning is concerned with these meaning associations added by speakers and cultures. One very important element of this is called *pragmatics*, which is the study of how speakers and writers use the resources of communication to convey intended meanings. When you encounter language, you not only use the conventional meanings of the words, but you try to figure out what the speaker intends. You try to figure out what the speaker is trying to do. This is sometimes referred to as "invisible meaning" because you must use assumptions, contexts, background information, and cultural knowledge that is not apparent to figure out the meaning. What if you are driving down the street and you see a sign that says "YARD SALE." Do you assume that someone is selling yards? Or, if the sign said "TAG SALE," would you think someone was selling tags? On the contrary, you know what these signs mean from your personal experiences in the culture. You know that someone has collected lots of different items and is selling them at very low prices. There will probably be old clothes, books, baby items, and used furniture. These words (old clothes, books, etc.) and the idea that someone is selling these things in their yard or garage at cheap prices do not appear in the simple sign. But our normal interpretation of how the creator of the sign intended the message makes understanding possible and simple.

We examine more issues related to pragmatics in chapters 5, 6, and 7. Also, at the end of this chapter, we consider additional interesting issues about meaning such as metaphors, vocabulary, and how new words are formed. But first, we must learn more details about structural semantics.

Structural Semantics

The branch of semantics that is the most formal and logical is called *structural semantics*. Structural semantics is a formal logic that many people have difficulty understanding because so little of our everyday use of language is comparable to formal logic. The purpose of structural semantics is to specify how sentences come to be true given the words in the language and the way in which the syntax organizes the words. Logicians claim that natural language can be expressed in a form of logic. The goal is to take the components of a sentence and provide a precise translation into the logic.

Structural semantics does not produce meaning for words; rather, it produces a complex expression of objects. The theory begins with a model that includes an *object language*. The object language pertains to the specific objects that parts of the natural language refer to. Thus, the name for something, such as house, will refer to a set of objects (the class of houses) that it denotes. Structural semantics assumes that meanings have already been assigned to words. The theory is not concerned with the actual determination of meaning or providing clues to common usage. The particular objects of a sentence must then be organized according to a syntax. The component parts and the way in which they are organized determine the meaning of a sentence. There is a corresponding semantic rule for each syntactic rule. These rules are a metalanguage that allow for statements regarding the object language. They are comparable to syntactic rules that we encountered earlier such as S → NP + VP, which means that a sentence (on the left side of the equation) can be rewritten as a rule on the right side of the equation, or as being composed of a noun phrase and a verb phrase. The semantic rule would be as follows: The sentence is true if the object(s) expressed by the noun phrase is/are in particular relation to the object(s) denoted by the verb phrase. So the sentence "Steve hits" is true if there is someone called Steve and he hits.

Semantics and Truth. In structural semantics, a semantic theory is a theory of truth. A goal of semantic theory is to state that something is true or false, and to do that, we must distinguish between sentences in a language that are *linguistically true* and those that are *empirically true*. A sentence is determined to be linguistically true if its truth is established by its structure and semantics of the language and not by checking facts in the empirical world. A sentence is empirically true if we must confirm it by checking the empirical world as to its correctness. Most communication is of this latter type. If I say "My briefcase is on the desk," then the sentence is empirically true if the briefcase is actually on the desk. But consider the following sentences and note how it is possible to establish their truth value without reference to the empirical world:

1. The window is either open or it is not open.
2. If Don and Bob like baseball, then Don likes baseball.
3. The window is open and it is closed. (False)

These sentences are called *analytical sentences* because their truth value is determined by logical connectives such as "either," "if," and "then." Sentences 1 and 2 are true and Sentence 3 is false. We can see that the form of these sentences makes them true and not their empirical content. They can be cast as logical equations because Sentences 1 and 2 can take the forms:

4. Either S or not-S.
5. If S and S′, then S.

but Sentence 3 is false because the following equation cannot be true:

6. S and not-S.

The sentences in Examples 1–3 are true or false because the words "either," "and," and "if" are logical terms that dictate how one part of a sentence should relate to another. But in the following sentences, terms are descriptive of certain subject matter and although it is possible to generate their logical forms, it is also possible to produce false sentences:

7. If Bill is a genius, then he is intelligent.
8. If the perfume was fragrant, then it was scented.
9. If Bill is a genius, then he is dumb.

Sentences 7 and 8 are true and Sentence 9 is false. The first two sentences are true because the key terms each imply one another. To be a genius is by definition to be intelligent, and anything that has a fragrance has a scent. In Sentence 9, we have related two terms that cannot be true, so the sentence is false. These three sentences can be cast into logical forms quite easily:

10. If Bill is G, then Bill is I.
11. If perfume was F, then it was S.
12. If Bill is G, then Bill is not D.

The types of sentences in Examples 7–9, and their logical forms in 10–12, are called analytic sentences because they are true by virtue of their structural nature.

Entailment.   One other function of a theory of truth and semantics is *entailment*. Simply, entailment means "follow from" or that the truth of one sentence guarantees the truth of a second as in Examples 13 and 14:

13. Bill is a man *entails* Bill is a mammal.

14. Karen awoke at 5:30 *entails* Karen was asleep immediately prior to
5:30.

Logical entailment is a goal of a formal theory of semantics, but it is often
difficult to achieve because the logic of semantic structure is not always
clear. Words such as "man" and "mammal" or "color" and "blue" imply one
another and can be written as analytical sentences. The language of some
natural sciences (e.g., chemistry, physics) begins to approximate the type
of semantic precision necessary for exact description and analysis. The specificity of the language used to describe a chemical process, for example, and
the close relation between a term and its referent, makes it possible for
these sciences to be more exact. Some sentences do not easily entail others,
such as Example 15 does not necessarily entail Example 16:

15. Don cleaned the house.
16. The house was clean.

There are situations in which Example 15 would be true but 16 would not
be, because it is possible for Don to engage in house-cleaning activities but
have the house still not be what we would call clean.

The types of sentences in Examples 15 and 16 are more like the sentences
in natural language during communication because the meanings of words
change according to usage patterns and individuals. Because it is not possible
to have an objective measure of a clean house, or a definition that would
represent complete consensus, Sentence 16 cannot be an entailment of 15.
In short, very little of our everyday language takes the form of logic that
can be expressed in a formula. Formal logic and theories of truth have really
very little relevance to natural languages—that is, little relevance to the way
people actually use language. This is because sentence comprehension also
requires general knowledge about the world: It requires individual language
users to bring background information and presuppositions that are necessary for comprehension. It is important to underscore that structural semantics has solved certain problems in linguistics and is quite useful for recognizing where literal meaning ends and inferences using background
information begin. Literal and conventional meaning has been the province
of traditional linguistics, and context sensitive meaning is in the realm of
pragmatics and communication.

The gap between formal logic and natural language has been bridged
by developments in two areas. The first is contextual semantics, which is
so central to communication that we take it up in chapter 5 and various
remaining chapters. Contextual semantics is about how people actually use
language (communicate) and assign meaning to utterances that are not truth
conditional. But within the realm of logic, perhaps the most important con-

cept for semantics was that of *possible worlds* (Kripke, 1963). This work emerges from work with possibilities, probabilities, beliefs, and so on. The concept of possible worlds makes it possible for a statement not to be true or false but true or false within a possible world. The sentence

17. It is possible that David is friendly.

is true if there is at least one possibility that the sentence

18. David is friendly.

is true. This helps with the application of semantic theories to natural language. Structural semantics has little bearing on actual language use and communication. And the reason for this, as we have seen, is that the logical structure of formulae does not correspond well to natural language and that the proper unit of analysis might not be the sentence.

Lexical Semantics

Lexical semantics is the study of word meanings. In the formal theories of structural semantics, the meaning of a word is assigned (e.g., "book" denotes a set of books), and truth conditions result from logical formulae or the structural relations between words. But lexical semantics must explain how people understand words and what cognitive processes interact with this understanding to produce meaningful communication.

The earliest work in lexical semantics was inspired by transformational grammar. In Chomsky's first book (1957), he did not even mention issues in semantics. But in his second book (Chomsky, 1965), he proposed what is known as standard theory. Standard theory builds on ideas proposed by Katz and Fodor (1963), in which they stipulated that meaning can be described as a set of *features* that define a word. The communication theorist and linguist are concerned with the concept of a word. There is no single thing, for example, that is a *dog*. The word "dog" refers to a concept or a sense in which things belong to a conceptual class called "dog." A word spoken in an actual communication situation is only a single instance of a meaning, but it is the underlying sense of the word that defines the instance as correct or appropriate. We need to have a lexicon (dictionary) and rules for combining words.

Katz and Fodor (1963) suggested that each entry in our cognitive lexicon was defined according to features (markers) of the entry compared to all other entries. There would be a marker for every meaning associated with a word. The word "drill," for example, would have one semantic marker for the concept of "machine that makes a hole," and another marker for "routine practice." A further example might help by explaining the way in which the words "woman" and "man" would be defined and distinguished by the semantic system. We would say that a woman was "human" (expressed as +HUMAN) and +ADULT, +ANIMATE, +FEMALE. A man would be +HUMAN, +ADULT, +ANIMATE, +MALE. All semantic markers apply to both except the +MALE and + FEMALE distinction. The markers specify both their similarity and differences. The markers also state how "man" and "woman" are more similar to each other than they are to "drill," for example.

After enumerating all semantic markers for the lexical items in the language, the theory still needs rules to state what syntactical combinations are permissible. The rules must lead to acceptable grammatical sentences and be specific enough not to produce sentences such as "The drill is thinking about dinner," because inanimate objects do not have cognitive capabilities. A sentence such as "The man is thinking about dinner" would be acceptable.

Semantic feature theories were used to account for word association tests. McNeill and McNeill (1968) argued that if word meanings were made up of sets of features, then people were most likely to respond to a stimulus word with one that had many features in common. Moreover, their arguments were bolstered by findings that children were more able to associate words that are naturally related rather than purely semantically related. So a child would see "deep" and "hole" as more related than "deep" and "shallow," because deep–hole is a natural relation.

Feature theories were also influenced by the research on memory for sentences. A number of researchers (e.g., Sachs, 1967) found that the semantic message of a sentence is what people remember about sentences, and the syntactic structure fades quickly. If participants were exposed to a sentence such as "The rock was small," they were likely to recognize the sentence "The rock was not big" as one they had seen before. Clark and Clark (1968) thought that markedness could explain sentence memory experiments. They argued that when people heard words and sentences, they extracted semantic distinctions in the form of features. Recall of sentences was assumed to be a reconstruction of semantic features.

WORDS, MEANINGS, AND MINDS

This section explains some properties of words and their meanings. The purpose is to show that meanings have more to them than logical relations and sets of features; they are the result of intricate relations between the language system, human psychology, and culture. In this section, we explore certain universal aspects of meaning and how this leads to categorization of the things in the world. From here, we examine the Sapir–Whorf hypothesis, followed by various components of meaning, and the principal ways that new words come into existence.

Linguistic Relativity

Words do not refer to a single "thing." They do not relate directly to the world, but flow through our minds. This means that words are subject to all of the conditions of the mind, including a speaker's attitudes and culture. This point is very clear to anyone who has learned a second language. All sorts of issues about family, kinship, gender, and respect are coded into a language, and learning a second language becomes confusing when the rules change. In English, the second-person pronoun "you" is the same whether you are addressing a male or female. But in Hebrew, for example, gender is coded into the second-person pronouns and they are different depending on whether you are speaking to a male or female. English speakers have trouble mastering all the terms of respect in Japanese.

Terms for colors are a very good example of how the world is not divided into neat objective categories that words can capture. You might think that colors are fairly objective, that they are essentially expressible in physical terms of light and wavelength, and so forth. You might also assume that colors are the same everywhere: that red is red in the United States or China. It turns out that things are not this simple: Speakers of different languages may see colors in very different ways.

Russian has two words for "blue": *sinij* (dark blue) and *goluboy* (sky blue). Important research by Berlin and Kay (1969) explained that the basic color terms can be grouped across all languages, as shown in Fig. 4.1. It turns out that all languages have terms for "black" and "white." Next comes the word for "red." This too is a term in almost all languages. A language called Tiv in Nigeria bases all its color terms on variations of these three. The arrow in Fig. 4.1 indicates the progression of acquiring words for these colors. This scale captures how languages adopt color terms, because a language will have all the terms to the left of a color but not necessarily to the right. So the Navahos have terms for "green" and "yellow" and everything to the left but not to the right. If a Navaho encounters the color "pink," it is described in terms other than single, basic color terms.

English, of course, uses many color terms every day that have modifications of some sort. Terms such as "eggshell white," "hot pink," "navy blue,"

black	red	green	blue	brown	purple
white		yellow			pink
					orange
					gray

FIG. 4.1. Basic color terms according to Berlin and Kay (1969).

"autumn gold," and "burnt orange" include the meaning of other terms. These "colors" are the result of aggressive advertising, marketing, clothing stores, and paint stores where the goal is to create a highly specific feel and mood for the colors. Results of studies on colors indicate considerable agreement when participants are asked to identify basic colors such as red, black, and yellow but much less agreement on highly modified colors, such as the difference between "sky blue," "royal blue," "seaside blue," "azure blue," and "navy blue."

Color words show how similar all languages are with respect to basic colors because of human perception. But they also show how different cultures choose to organize and express color terms. Some cultures use very few color variations, and others use many. Color terms are an example of how members of a culture categorize the world. An American paint store owner might genuinely "see" the color "burnt orange," whereas someone in another culture would never describe any color this way. They literally do not see any such color.

This notion of categorizing the world with language leads to additional issues of how language relates to thinking. It is sensible to assume that different languages lead to different ways of seeing and categorizing the world. If English has a word for "burnt orange," then speakers of English recognize it. There is a well-known hypothesis called the Sapir–Whorf hypothesis that makes just such a point (Whorf, 1956). This hypothesis maintains that the nature and structure of one's language determine their perceptions of the world. Whorf (1956) studied other cultures, especially the Hopi Indians, and discovered that the Hopi had one word, *pahe*, for drinking water and another word, *keyi*, for natural water in lakes. He also claimed that the Hopi had different conceptions of time than standard Europeans such that the Hopi tended to see things as always in a state of becoming. The literal Hopi translation of a sentence such as "John is a student" would be "John is becoming a student." All of this was supposed to demonstrate that Hopi language carved up the world in a particular way, and this determined how the Hopi saw and understood the world. Probably the most famous example of the Sapir–Whorf hypothesis is that Eskimos have numerous words for "snow" compared to the single word in English.

There has been much controversy over the Sapir–Whorf hypothesis. It is simply not true that just because a language has multiple ways of expressing an idea or concept, other languages are deficient at such expressions. The Hopi are certainly capable of expressing and understanding different conceptions of time. They just do it differently with their language. And English speakers can express all the types of snow that the Eskimos can: In English we can say "wet snow," "slush," "hail," "dirty snow," and "powder." An English speaker can see and understand all the types of snow that the Eskimo sees and understands. Still, it is efficient for a language to have specialized ways of referring to things that are important. Snow is obviously more important in the life of an Eskimo than it is to someone who lives in Hawaii. Over time, a language evolves toward more efficient and specialized expressions, but this does not mean that speakers of another language are incapable of understanding these concepts.

Parsing Meaning

There are numerous ways to divide up or "parse" meaning. Words tend to group into families and constitute a meaning on the basis of semantic features as described earlier. For example, food and nourishment are divided up into things we eat and things we drink. Anything we drink is liquid, and things we eat are nonliquid. So the noun "drink" has the meaning component +LIQUID and the noun "food" is –LIQUID. Drinks are also usually either hot or cold. So "tea," "soup," and "coffee" are +LIQUID, +HOT, and "Coke," "lemonade," and "gin and tonic" are +LIQUID, –HOT. Drinks can also be either alcoholic or nonalcoholic. Thus, "tea" and "coffee" are +LIQUID, +HOT, –ALCOHOLIC, and "beer" and "gin and tonic" are +LIQUID, –HOT, +ALCOHOLIC.

Meaning can build in these ways. It is possible to violate the usual meaning of something, but the violation is usually coded into the language. Tea can be +COLD, but then it is termed "iced tea." Coffee can be +COLD, but then it is "iced coffee." Soup can be +COLD, but it is labeled "cold soup." All of these terms have additional meanings to fill out the details. The coffee can be + or – CAFFEINATED, + or – GOURMET, + or – STRONG, and so forth. Not everyone can make all of these distinctions or knows the difference between gourmet and nongourmet coffee. But we all use these meaning components to organize our understanding of the word and to distinguish one word from another at our own level of knowledge. If all coffee is the same to me, then I have no + or – GOURMET category. That is not a distinction that is meaningful to me. But if you are a coffee connoisseur, then the meaning of the word "coffee" does contain a GOURMET category.

Wine Terms.   The family of words for wine can be very interesting and can be captured through the feature components we have been discussing. As knowledge of wine has grown, so has the terminology and number of complex distinctions that can be made. The following example is for only one set of meaning components, and they are not completely exhaustive.

Is the wine +RED or +WHITE? If it is +RED, then where did it come from? Is it +FRENCH, +ITALIAN, or +CALIFORNIA? If it is French, is it +BORDEAUX or +BURGUNDY? If it is +BORDEAUX, which territory does it come from? Is it +MÉDOC, +BAS-MÉDOC, +ST-ESTÈPHE, +ST-JULIEN,

+MARGAUX, or some other lesser region? What is the wine's quality? Is it +ORDINARY, +VIN DE PAYS, +GOOD, +FINE, or +GREAT? When a growing season is so good that the wine does not have to be blended, the wine is classified as a vintage. Is the wine +VINTAGE or –VINTAGE? The various wines in the +BORDEAUX region are classified as +CLASSIC (the best), +BOURGEOIS (those wines a little behind classic), and +ARTISAN (wines of moderate quality). The +BOURGEOIS wines are graded as *crus exceptionnels, crus bourgeois supérieures,* and *crus bourgeois.* So each of the bourgeois wines can be + or – one of the *crus* categories.

The next time you go into a nice restaurant and order a bottle of Château Margaux, tell the wine steward you want +RED, +FRENCH, +BORDEAUX, +CHÂTEAU MARGAUX, and you even want +VINTAGE. You will not need to say +CLASSIC, because that meaning is also part of the +CHÂTEAU MARGAUX. Oh yes, you also will not have to say +EXPENSIVE!

The meanings of these terms are made up of the components. As usual, there are always areas of ambiguity and confusion as well as additional detail. If you read the wine column in a newspaper or magazine, you will see many words used to describe wine. Each of the following can be either + or – and contributes to the meaning of "wine": balanced, flowery, sweet, dry, tart, young, gentle, bouquet, perfumed, bitter. Meaning components are a useful way of describing the meaning of words. When children are developing language, they develop the components in a relatively systematic fashion: They develop the most basic components first and more precise distinctions later.

New Words

New words sometimes find their way into a language because a very creative person has simply invented a new word. However, this is extremely rare because a new word—completely unrelated to any other word—would reflect a new reality, and that is very difficult. Moreover, one can make up new words, but they have to be accepted. They have to find their way into regular usage, and this too is extremely difficult. Words do not have individual meaning so much as they enter into relations with other words. They are part of a family of meanings that share components with other words. It is best not to think of words as having a single meaning but as contrasting with other words in the language. Therefore, almost all new words are really new uses or new word formations based on old words. They all share some minimal meaning components. There are primarily five ways that new words are formed:

1. One of the simplest ways to form a new word is to add a prefix. The prefix *tele* means "at a distance." The word *phone* means "sound," so a telephone is "sound at a distance." Now, anything done at a distance

can include the prefix *tele*. Vision at a distance is *tele-vision*, making phone calls to sell a product is called *tele-marketing*. If you work from your computer at home and connect up with others at the office, you are *tele-commuting*. Some prefixes have fixed meanings that can be used frequently. *Anti* means "against" and *pro* means "for." One can be *anti* anything: *anti-school, anti-work, anti-semitic, anti-housework, anti-government,* and so forth. The same is true for *pro*.

2. Suffixes are another simple way to form words. A suffix is an addition to the end of a word that changes the meaning of a word and its grammatical category. A simple example is the suffix *er* that makes a word an agentive noun; that is, the person who does something. *Hit* becomes *hitter, throw* becomes *thrower,* and *walk* becomes *walker*. You can add the suffix *able* to many verbs and make a word that means "able to be X'd," where X is the meaning of the verb. *Wash* becomes *washable*. Of course, not all verbs can take *able*. The verb *die* does not become *dieable*, and *sleep* does not become *sleepable*. There are many prefixes and suffixes that alter the meaning of words. Learning how these work is part of becoming competent in the grammar of a language.

3. Another way to create a new word is by compounding. This is simply adding two different words together to make a new word. Words such as *disc jockey* and *downsizing* are compounds. The word *micro* means small and detailed and indicates the inner workings of something. We have the words *micromanage, microchip,* and *microchemistry*. There is always some question as to whether or not to use a hyphen for compound words. When two words are first formed, they usually take a hyphen (e.g., *baby-talk*) but over time, the hyphen drops out as the two words are combined. Compounding is very common and is found in all languages. One particularly strong adherent of animal communication has argued that chimps can form new words in the same way when they learn sign language. A chimp once saw a duck land on the water in a lake and signed a *water-bird*.

4. A fourth way to make words do new things is to change their grammatical class. Changing nouns into verbs is probably the most typical example. The word *memo* was historically a noun. One wrote or read a memo. But now you will hear some people say, "*Memo* me on that." A *pocket* is something on a pair of pants, but one can *pocket* the money, meaning "to put the money in a pocket."

5. Infixes are the final way to create new words and meaning. Infixes are rare in English but more common in some other language. Infixes occur when you add something to the middle of a word. In English, they are associated with casual slang and you would rarely see them

written. If I want to emphasize something in a very assertive way, I might say *abso-damn-lutely*. The *damn* is inserted in the middle of the word *absolutely*.

Certainly the interesting questions about meaning and communication are not truth conditional or based solely on feature theories of meaning. In the sentence "The woman went to see the divorce lawyer," there is no entailment between the woman's own marital status and her visiting a divorce lawyer. Although one would typically assume this relation, there are contexts in which the woman might be visiting a friend or doing an interview for a magazine. Communication theorists must explain how our knowledge of the world is organized and accessed by linguistic and textual cues. The next two chapters are devoted to discussing contemporary theories and ideas of meaning and how these relate to the process of communication.

CHAPTER FIVE

Pragmatics and Discourse

We ended the previous chapter by suggesting that the concept of meaning was reliant on generalized knowledge and communicative use. People speak to individuals or groups for different reasons, and the language fulfills different functions. A speaker may say, "Hey, what's happenin' " to a friend just to make contact or pronounce you "man and wife" in a formal and legal ceremony. All of these uses of language are instrumental for human communication and part of the general theory of pragmatics.

PRAGMATICS

The use of knowledge about the world and how your language works to understand texts, either oral or written, is the study of language practices or *pragmatics*. If language use (actual communication) determines meaning, then a theory of semantics must incorporate these principles. Chomsky showed how a speaker was linguistically competent; that is, had innate knowledge about the structure of language. But we would surely want to consider any of the following as part of a speaker's linguistic and communicative competence:

1. *What's happenin'* can be a greeting.
2. *Where's my computer?* is a question.
3. *Where's my computer?* is an accusation.

4. *I promise to mow your lawn* is a genuine commitment to mow my lawn.

5. *Is that your coat on the floor?* is not a question but an order to pick it up.

6. *It's hot today* is a statement that it's hot.

7. *This sandwich is mine* correctly refers to a particular object that I possess.

Pragmatics is the study of how communicators use a context to come to conclusions about meaning. Speakers and writers mean things that are not stated explicitly in language. To be understood, they must rely on the assumptions and skills of listeners and readers. Senders of messages always depend on a certain amount of knowledge that receivers of messages carry around. Skilled communicators know, for example, how to draw conclusions from what speakers say and how to use the context to fulfill meaning. In a sense, pragmatics refers to invisible meaning—the assumptions behind a message. If I uttered the statement in Example 5 to my daughter, it would be heard by her as an order and not a genuine question about the ownership of the coat. Pragmatics emphasizes the influence of context, which is treated briefly later, but then concerns itself primarily with the linguistic aspects of interpretations (as opposed to the cognitive ones treated in chap. 3): speech act theory and implicatures. All of these are discussed next.

Context

The discourse analyst Teun van Dijk (1997) wrote that context is what "we need to know about in order to properly understand the event, action or discourse" (p. 11). Karen Tracy (1998) explained how difficult and convoluted the concept of context can be. The concept of context is rather like the concept of communication: It is complex and difficult, yet we use it effortlessly every day. Perhaps one of the best ways to think about the idea of "context" is in terms of a figure–ground relation (Goodwin & Duranti, 1992). A word draws our attention to it, but that word has a relation with a background. That background necessary for interpreting the word is context.

Context is perhaps the most important element of pragmatic analysis. First, there is the *linguistic context,* which is the collection of words in a sentence or phrase that helps determine what each of them can mean. The word "check," for example, has more than one meaning. In the sentence "Jim paid the check and left," it draws primarily on the implication of the word "paid" to conclude that "check" refers to the bill in a restaurant. But if the sentence were "Write me a check," the word would mean something else. The *physical context* is simply the collection of people and objects that constitutes the time and place in which communication occurs. If I see the word "check" on the wall of a bank, it will cause me to come to a different interpretation than if I see the word near a room that stores hats and coats in a restaurant.

INTERPRETATION AND REFERENCE

What types of interpretation are involved in typical discourse processing? A communicator provides a respondent with input data in the form of text, which is composed of surface features (e.g., vocabulary, syntactic structures), paraverbal cues (gestural and visual signals), and contextual information. There are a number of particular textual and contextual mechanisms that contribute to interpretation. But our concern here is with the general problems that a respondent must solve to interpret any communication. Sanders (1981, 1987) has been working on these problems and concluded that three types of meaning must be established. This meaning is the result of interpretations regarding (a) propositional content of utterances, (b) illocutionary force, and (c) implicatures. These meaning types, especially illocutionary force and implicatures, are sensitive to problems in meaning that require context. They represent attempts to incorporate background knowledge into semantic theories.

Language users make interpretations on the basis of any combination of three principles:

1. *Routine modes of interpretation that are presupposed.* These are methods of deciding how to draw inferences, most notably implicatures that are not logically entailed.
2. *Mechanisms in the language and culture that cause people to focus on the structures of a discourse necessary to ensure that the discourse is coherent;* that is, that antecedent and subsequent components of the discourse can be related. This includes *reference* or how a speaker enables a listener to identify something.
3. *Individual and idiosyncratic understanding of the people involved in the communication.* People form relationships with private codes and modes of understanding that can be used to establish understanding. These are based on an individual's habits and dispositions.

These types of interpretations cannot be completely separated from one another. They are normally complementary but may be treated individually for the sake of clarity. In the following, we focus on the issues inherent in Principle 1. We explore the issues related to Principle 2 in the next chapter. These are the principles that extend theories of semantics to pragmatic communication and are the most important theoretically. The judgments individuals make on the basis of their own interpretive schemes are usually highly variable, difficult to ascertain, and of limited applicability. Moreover, idiosyncratic interpretations can often be subsumed by Principles 1 and 2.

When faced with a piece of spoken or written communication, a listener or reader must interpret the communication in order to establish three types of meaning: propositional meaning, illocutionary force, and conventional implicatures. These types of meanings must be worked out of any and every communication. They are sometimes difficult, sometimes easy, sometimes ambiguous, sometimes dependent on one another, but always a part of the semantic problems to be solved when trying to create understanding.

Propositional Meaning

The propositional content of a communication is its meaning, derived solely on the basis of lexical content and syntactic structure arranged and used to express the content and relations implied by the language and how it is ordered. In the sentence

1. Michael Jordan is a Bull.

the propositional content refers to two entities (Michael Jordan and Bull), a relation between them (team and player), and a situation in which that relation is sensible. The propositional content is derived from the vocabulary and the syntactic relations that instruct the hearer or reader as to the relations among vocabulary terms. Propositional meaning is the most elementary meaning.

Processing the propositional content is a necessary first step in establishing the final meaning of an utterance. One cannot begin to understand Sentence 1 if one does not understand the terminology and the relation among terminological items. The theoretical problem alluded to is whether or not this understanding requires background knowledge or simply truth conditions. As we develop our ideas in this chapter, we see that a complete and accurate understanding of a discourse requires the listener or reader to apply world knowledge and cognitive schemas to the language in question. In Sentences 2–5, the verb "hit" refers to substantially different things, but the different uses of the term are not coded into the nature of the verb. One is required to have general knowledge about the world to understand the different uses for "hit."

2. John hit the ball.
3. John hit Bill.
4. John hit a jackpot.
5. John hit the rack. (went to bed)

It is also the case that both the literal and more metaphoric meanings of "hit" each imply some "striking action," whether it be a bed, a jackpot, or another person. So truth-conditional principles of semantics can account for some essential components of meaning, but they are insensitive to the future meanings that interpreters routinely apply.

There is still debate as to whether or not pragmatic meanings are required for a full semantic interpretation of an utterance (see, e.g., Gazdar, 1979; Posner, 1980; Sanders, 1987). But we take the position here that pragmatically informed content is an inherent part of any communicative use of language. Sanders claimed that only semantic oddities require pragmatic grounds to fully interpret a sentence. In Sentence 6, Sanders (1987, p. 56) suggests that a full understanding is metaphoric.

6. Getting pregnant and getting married is worse than getting married and getting pregnant.

The truth conditions of the sentence are such that there is no difference between "getting pregnant and getting married" and "getting married and getting pregnant," regardless of the order, but the comparative "worse than" presupposes that the two are not identical. Moreover, the communicative purpose of the utterance is to indicate that the order in which one gets pregnant and married certainly has consequences. The connective "and" is a linguistic indication that the order is important. But it is pragmatic meaning that accounts for a full interpretation of the sentence. As stated earlier, propositional content is still basic to understanding the sentences, because the vocabulary and syntax carry necessary meaning and information about the essential content of the communication.

It is possible, however, to view propositional content as dependent on background knowledge that people have about the world. Searle (1969, 1974) demonstrated that a sentence cannot be specified (truth-conditionally) without reference to pragmatic knowledge. Searle would argue that Sentences 2–5 are substantially different and cannot be compared even with a generalized semantic specification of "hit." His essential argument is that a person's knowledge of meaning is made up of a person's knowledge about how to *use* language and make sentences, clauses, questions, promises, demands, and so forth, and that people use sentences and utterances for a particular purpose. In other words, the key mistake made by Chomsky, feature theorists, and structural semanticists is that they fail to see the essential connection between language and communication. This important point is explained in more detail in the following section.

Illocutionary Force

The propositional content of utterances is used by speakers to signal *illocutionary acts*. This is a second type of meaning in communication. A listener must not only understand the basic references for words and syntactical relations, but he or she must understand how an utterance is functioning. If a sign says *Attack Dog on Premises*, this is a warning about how you should behave, not a simple statement describing the nature of the animal nearby. Illocutionary acts are utterances that have social and communicative purposes. Austin (1962) and Searle (1969) described *locutionary* acts as utterances with sense and reference, akin to propositional content. But an illocutionary act describes the function of the utterance. A speech act has illocutionary force when it does something: announce, promise, state, assert, command, request, propose, suggest, order, and so on. Austin pointed out that utterances also have *perlocutionary* effects; that is, effects on a hearer that are not part of the meaning of an utterance. The utterance "Go home!" is a locutionary act because it is well formed and makes a sensible reference to something. But it is also an illocutionary act that if said by the right person in the right context functions as an *order*. If the illocutionary act is successful and someone is sent to their place of residence, then the illocutionary act plus the consequences constitute perlocutionary effects.

Speech act theory and Gricean (1975, 1978) pragmatics are the major strands of linguistic work that successfully incorporate generalized knowledge about the communication system and its functions into semantics. Searle's (1969, 1974) primary objective was to show that propositional content is not very important and that illocutionary acts instruct an interpreter about how to use the content of an expression. This is significant, because it amounts to a rejection of the notion that there are context-free meanings—meanings that can be separated from speaker goals and intentions and the generalized knowledge of an interpreter. Searle realized that important elements of meaning went considerably beyond literal meaning. It also means that communication is the fundamental unit of semantic analysis, not an abstract and rarefied system of features and markers. Semantic competence is a matter of knowing relations between semantic intentions, rules, and situations. If a speaker says "This book is big," a hearer knows that it was said with the intention of making a statement and having a certain impact on the hearer. Searle's principal objection to Chomskyian semantics was that Chomsky treats language as an autonomous system only incidentally used for communication. Language is essentially a system of communication and it is therefore impossible to separate the communicative functions of language from accounts of the meaning of a sentence or utterance.

This weds discourse and semantics and blurs the often used distinction between competence and performance. A theory of meaning is a theory of communication and social action. Competence with the language implies a competence to perform. A language user must know more than grammatical rules and word meanings to use and understand a language competently. He or she must also know when and how to speak, to whom, in what situations, and for what desired effect. There is now a pragmatic orientation to the previously theoretical components of language.

Speech Act Semantics. Detailed examples of Searlean analyses of speech acts are readily available (see Searle, 1969, 1975), and we are brief here; nevertheless, it is important to demonstrate speech act analysis to show how principles of pragmatics and communication are necessary aspects of meaning. A set of rules that constitute a speech act and provide an account of how one type of meaning is produced is given here. The theoretical concern is how one discovers a set of rules that govern the use of language. Searle (1969) produced a strategy whereby we set down conditions on an illocutionary act such that if the conditions are met, the act is performed. These conditions must be recognized by both the speaker and hearer, which means that the purpose of the communicative exchange is fundamental to a complete semantic account. Searle used the performative verb "to promise" as an example.

Assume that someone utters the following:

7. I promise to mow your lawn.

What we have here is that Speaker S promised that he would do Act A for Hearer H. For our analysis to be successful, we need to explicate the rules and conditions that make it possible for competent language users to understand the utterance as a literal and sincere promise. We assume that both S and H (speaker and hearer) are engaged in normal communication such that there are no impediments: that both are conscious, capable of speaking and hearing the language, and so on. Searle (1969) identified four conditions necessary to perform promising.

The most basic ingredient of a promise—what separates it from other speech act functions—is that the speaker assumes an obligation to do something. The fact that a speaker does not fulfill his or her promise does not jeopardize the performance of a sincere promise. If I promise to mow your lawn but my lawn mower breaks down, I have not failed to perform or communicate a promise, I have failed to keep it. This is called the *essential condition: Speaker S is obligated to do Act A.*

A second ingredient of a genuine promise is that the speaker plans to honor the promise. Again, a speaker's failure to honor a promise does not change the nature of the act. If, however, a speaker never intended to keep his or her promise, he or she is not promising genuinely or sincerely. This then is another act called "lying." This second fact is called the *sincerity condition: Speaker S has every intention of doing Act A.*

A third necessary rule for promising is the belief by the speaker that the hearer wants the promised act performed. The speaker must believe that it is in the hearer's interest to do Act A. A violation of this rule is one way to distinguish between a promise and a threat. If I say to a friend, "Pay me the money you owe me or I promise legal action," then I am not actually "promising," I am "threatening." This is called the *preparatory condition: Speaker S believes doing Act A is in Hearer H's best interest.*

Finally, there is the *propositional content condition: Speaker S predicates a future Act A.* This means that the speaker will do something him- or herself, something in particular such as mow the lawn, pay the money he or she owes, or whatever. A speaker cannot just promise anything; rather, it must be something he or she can perform and meets the conditions of promising.

The example we have just enumerated illustrates the extent to which semantics is dependent on the role of communicators and their assumptions about the world. If all the conditions are met, then a promise has been made, but we can see how violating certain conditions accounts for different meanings of the same words, an issue that semanticists have grappled with for a long time. Violating the preparatory condition turns a promise into a threat. Violating the sincerity condition makes for a lie. And I can capitalize on the essential condition of promising in statements such as "I promise I didn't take your money," which is not a genuine promise but an indication that I am very committed to my statement.

The rules taken together *constitute* promising in the same way that the rules of basketball or chess constitute these games. Basketball and chess do not have an existence separate from their rules. Their rules bring them into existence. The rules of basketball and chess, just to use these examples, stipulate all of the legitimate moves and possibilities. The rules of promising or any other performative verb constitute how to perform these communicative acts. And people learn these rules while they are learning language. One part of learning a language is learning pragmatic rules, such as the ones for promising. It is easy to see how a speaker's intention to promise can be recognized by a hearer. The word "recognize" means to "re-cognize" or to invoke the perceptual and intellectual apparatus necessary for understanding. This is precisely what an individual does during communication: He or she uses the rules and conditions that he or she has acquired to make sense of the sounds of the other individual in the communication. So meaning in discourse or communication involves intentional language use formulated according to rules and principles acquired and understood by both a speaker and a hearer.

Speech Acts and Action. The theory of speech acts and the kind of meaning that interpretants extract from utterances that have illocutionary force are based on theories of action. Action theory is another way to describe how principles of natural language and discourse are dependent on assumptions other than truth conditional semantics. Sentences such as "There are blue birds" or "There are no blue birds" have rules for representing how the information is conveyed in such sentences. But when we do something other than assert sentences that can be verified, when we say things that function as requests, commands, promises, and so forth, proposals for truth conditions are bound to fail because they do not adequately account for all that is involved in the utterance. There are two reasons why this is true.

First, any utterance of natural language functions as a speech act in the broad sense of the term. Any single word, sentence fragment, or string of words functions first and foremost as purposeful human action. Natural language carries with it information about the context and thoughts of the speaker and hearer. There is no such thing as language that is "simply words"; rather, a sentence of any type is performed intentionally for a reason, on the basis of the speaker's goals and his or her beliefs about the available means of attaining goals. When I speak to someone, I have reliable beliefs and assumptions about how to use language under these circumstances. Dummett (1976) showed that understanding requires one to take into account assumptions about a speaker but also assumptions pertaining to the relation between language and the recipient of a message.

We can take it as a given that an explication of a speech act will not benefit by probing the physical qualities of an utterance. But all speech acts are characterized by goals, means to achieving goals, effects, and relationships. It would be possible to take any particular speech act and establish the connections between the text of the act and the goals of the utterance, strategic means for achieving the goal, relationships, or the effect. Kasher (1985) showed how this essentially makes any piece of natural language a type of discourse with communicative value. If I say to you "What is your name?" the goal of the utterance is simply to elicit your name from you. I have used standard question formation principles in the English language. I could also, however, have said any of the following: "What name do you go by?" "How are you called?" "Your appellation please?" "What's yer name buddy?" "How shall I address you sir?" These would all be different means to the same end and of course signal different attitudes and relationships. The individuals in a communication must also be knowledgeable about one another. If I say "I order you to leave the premises," I must be in the appropriate relational position to make such a statement. Outcomes of speech acts are more general results and consequences. The outcome of asking someone their name might be a developing friendship, an insult, or a suspicious glance. In short, language users internalize the issues and rules that preside over speech acts.

A second ingredient of the action perspective concerns the constitutive rules discussed earlier. Constitutive rules are vehicles for definitional justification. They are particularly important for semantic analyses of discourse because of the functional nature of discourse. The analogy between natural language and formal activity such as games is a useful one. Rules belong to a family of rules and a particular rule acquires its meaning by being a member of the family of rules. So the rule that specifies how to make a touchdown in football does so because it is part of the definition of the game. One cannot independently evaluate or explain the rule for making a touchdown; it makes sense only as part of the definition of football. The same is true for natural language. An explication and evaluation of an act of natural language can only take place within the family of rules and assumptions that govern the act. These types of rules are central to the semantics of discourse because they are derived from the meanings designated by language users. Discourses do not "have" meanings, but meanings are assigned by language users in some concrete interaction. Interpretation is something that people "do." The ability to perform speech acts results from learning how to make the correct interpretations. Because language use is not random or highly idiosyncratic, and knowing a language implies knowing how to use a language, the constitutive rules for a given act should be sufficiently clear for interpreters to identify the act.

Implicature

Implicature is a third pragmatic problem in meaning that must be solved by interpretants. Implicatures (Grice, 1975) are part of the problems that communicators must solve to accomplish understanding. They are part of inferencing in general. They are, as with interpreting propositional content and speech acts, guided by rules about what people need to know and must assume in order to make sense of or interpret messages.

Grice (1975) began with the assumption that conversation is a cooperative activity. He took it as a given that interaction is to a large degree concerted and orderly. He proposed that his cooperative principle is operative and that any deviation from the principle prompts inferences (p. 49). The cooperative principle is a general assumption held by all interactants that says that when formulating what to say, "make your conversational contribution such as is required, at the stage at which it occurs, by the accepted purpose or direction of the talk exchange in which you are engaged" (p. 45). This general maxim is supplemented by four submaxims that if adopted will contribute to a cooperative exchange. The four submaxims are as follows:

- *Quantity:* Make your contribution to a communication neither more nor less than is required.
- *Quality:* Be no more informative than is required. Say what you know to be true.

- *Relevancy:* Be relevant. Make your contribution in accordance with the context.
- *Manner:* Be brief, orderly, and avoid ambiguity. Avoid disorganization, verbosity, and obscurity.

When a communicator violates one of the maxims and is not cooperative, he or she invites *conversational implicature.* Generally speaking, a conversational implicature is an interpretive procedure that operates to figure out what is going on. For example, the following conversation violates the relevancy submaxim. Assume a husband and wife are getting ready to go out for the evening:

8. Husband: How much longer will you be?
9. Wife: Mix yourself a drink.

To interpret the utterance in Sentence 9, the husband must go through a series of inferences based on principles that he knows the other speaker is using. The husband assumes that the wife is being cooperative, even though she has violated the relevance principle. Remaining topical is a key function of the relevancy maxim, and the wife has violated the expectation that conversationalists extend the topic. The conventional response to the husband's question would be a direct answer where the wife indicated some time frame in which she would be ready. This would be a conventional implicature with a literal answer to a literal question. But the husband assumes that she heard his question, that she believes that he was genuinely asking how long she would be, and that she is capable of indicating when she would be ready. The wife could lie about how long she will be and violate the quality maxim, but instead she chooses not to extend the topic by ignoring the relevancy maxim. The husband then searches for a plausible interpretation of her utterance and concludes that what she is *doing* is telling him that she is not going to offer a particular time, or doesn't know, but she will be long enough yet for him to have a drink. She may also be saying, "Relax, I'll be ready in plenty of time."

What is implicated in discourse is not logically entailed by the utterance, so implicatures are an important solution to problems that cannot be solved by a semantic theory principally concerned with truth conditions and entailment. Implicatures have two defining features that make them particularly useful. First, they are cancelable. This means that attaching a clause or often even a word changes the meaning of an utterance. If two people are leaving a restaurant where they just paid an exorbitant bill and one says

10. That was inexpensive.

he or she is obviously violating the maxim of quality (tell the truth). As we explained earlier, the hearer will use a conversational implicature to work out the meaning and discover that the utterance has ironic intent. But an added clause as in Sentence 11 changes the meaning and importance of the utterance.

11. That was inexpensive, I really thought it was going to be worse.

Nondetachability is a second feature of conversational implicatures. This means that the implicature does not change when the same thing is said in different words. For example,

12. Some cheap meal, eh.

calls for the same implicature as in Sentence 10.

Conversational implicatures and their features are powerful mechanisms for interpretation because they model the competence that speakers must have to accomplish meaning. It is a strength of Gricean implicatures that they allow speakers and hearers to code assumptions and background knowledge into their decisions about meaning. As such, these implicatures are central to the semantics of discourse. If we examine implicatures a little more closely, we can see how the relation between form and content taps into the subjective state of individual interpreters. A conversational implicature relies on three things for interpretation: the propositional content, the particular maxim that has been violated, and the nature of the implication (Grice, 1975). We have talked about propositional content elsewhere in this chapter. It is the coordination of lexical and syntactic choices responsible for the inherent meaning of an utterance, meaning that does not include extralinguistic or additional understandings. But the second thing that an individual must recognize is the relation between the propositional content and the maxim.

Speakers must have an understanding about the general state of affairs to recognize that a conversational maxim has been violated. This means that interpretations about meaning and implicatures are based on a language user's cognitive models for general experience. To say that a speaker has violated a Gricean submaxim implies that the speaker has some subjective sense of what it means to be relevant, say just what is needed, say it clearly, and truthfully. There is an interaction, then, between propositional content and a speaker's cognitive models that produces the interpretation that a maxim has been violated (Sanders, 1987). Communicators assume common understandings and use these assumptions in decisions about meaning. Cicourel (1973) made important contributions to interpretive procedures by arguing that all language users have a "common scheme of reference" (p.

34), a set of interpretive procedures that are presupposed by everyone. One of these interpretive procedures is *reciprocity of perspectives* or that both parties to a communication are orienting toward the situation and the subject matter in the same way, a type of "common definition of the situation." This makes for a shared basis for knowing what attitudes, beliefs, and assumptions to use when interpreting an utterance. Perspectives on a situation are not completely reciprocal but sufficiently general to work out meaning. Interpreters who know one another very well have richer information than those who do not. But even complete strangers share membership in social, cultural, and linguistic groups such that they can apply common stereotypes. The exchange in Sentences 13 and 14 demonstrates the relation between propositional content and maxim violation:

13. You know, I could use some help moving on Saturday.
14. Saturday is my birthday.

The propositional content of Sentence 13 makes moving and all of the work related to moving salient. The fact that it is the hearer's birthday is irrelevant, but "sense" (cooperation) is restored when the speaker in Sentence 13 connects the belief that "one does not work on one's birthday, or has other plans" with the time and effort required to help someone move.

The content of the implicature is an interaction between the cognitive state of the individuals and the four submaxims stated earlier. For example, Sentence 16 violates the *quantity* submaxim because it is not informative enough:

15. I have some questions about a loan.
16. Here's a brochure.

Assuming the speaker in Sentence 16 is a bank officer and is knowledgeable about loans, there are reasons why he or she is not more forthcoming with information. Given the assumptions of the context and some norms about officials in institutions, the reply in Sentence 16 implicates that (a) the person does not want to be bothered and the speaker should leave him alone, (b) all questions can be answered by reading the brochure, or (c) read the brochure first and come back if you need additional information.

Other maxims or presumptions have been proposed as part of the reciprocal perspectives that communicators hold. These are assumed to generate inferences and interpretive procedures in the same way as Gricean maxims. Bach and Harnish (1979) suggested a "politeness maxim," a "morality maxim," and a "principle of charity." The politeness maxim invokes the speaker not to be rude, offensive, insulting, and the like. The morality maxim warns against communicating private or special information, requires the speaker not to do or say things that are forbidden, and so on. Finally, the principle of charity is a maxim that instructs hearers to assume that speakers do not violate very many maxims and give the speaker the benefit of the doubt whenever possible. The strength of the presuppositional overlap between a communicator and an interpreter is the primary determinant of implications. When the overlap is strong and there are minimal differences between communicators and interpreters, the likelihood of errors, misjudgments, and mistakes is diminished. By the same token, differences between people attributable to culture, language, competencies, or skills increase the chances for errors and uncoordinated communication.

DISCOURSE

In the previous section on pragmatics, we were mostly concerned with the particular relation between a sign (word or message) and its users. Pragmatics is confined to that specific relation between a communicator and how he or she uses a particular feature of language to construct meaning. Pragmatics typically focuses on vocabulary items, grammatical units, clauses, or sentences and the practical role they play in establishing meaning. Discourse, on the other hand, is language above the sentence or clause. There are many approaches to discourse (cf. Schiffrin, 1994), but all of them concern themselves with how language users make sense of what people say or what they read in texts. Listening to someone speak or reading a written document can be a confused and incoherent experience. But such is not usually the case, because discourse is organized in some way. The elements of a discourse are tied together and language users interpret these ties.

Traditional linguistics attempts to account for an isolated sentence or piece of language that is unconnected to behavior. The data consist of "well-formed sentences" that are independent of an individual speaker or his or her purposes. It is Chomsky's expressed desire to avoid the topic how language is used. The same is true for traditional linguistic semantics. The object of interest is a logical truth relation and not individual or social meaning. But when the unit of interest is a functional piece of language, then we are concerned with a discourse. *Discourse* is a general term that applies to either written or spoken language that is used for some communicative purpose. A discourse is a semantic concept. It is composed of text that is orderly according to interactional, cognitive, and linguistic principles. Within the tradition of linguistics, discourse is a concern for order in language beyond the sentence level. The discourse analyst is less concerned with formal properties of an abstract and isolated language and more interested in the communicative uses of language. Discourse is the intersection of language and communication. It is the point where the two disciplines meet.

Discourse is realized in text. *Text* is a string of language that carries the purposes of the discourse; it is, to be more precise, the lexico-grammatical expression of a speaker's or writer's functional goals. A communicator has options in meanings and makes choices about how to use and organize language to best serve his purposes. Halliday (1978) conceptualized "text" as functionally related to the environment because a speaker or writer's semantic system is activated by the environment, and the language and discourse is shaped by the environment. The relation between discourse and text is hierarchic because discourse is expressed in text. A discourse is a semantic system and a text is part of that system; the text is to the semantic system what a syllable is to the phonological system. But this hierarchical relation notwithstanding, the distinguishing feature of a semantic system is its organization into functional components, not units of different sizes. There are many structure-carrying units in discourse as well as grammar, and size is less important than purpose. A discourse can be a single utterance—even a single word—or a verbal exchange, a paragraph, a letter, a poster, a speech, an advertisement, a newspaper article, or any communicative use of language that serves some purpose.

Semantics, in the most general sense, is primarily concerned with the creation of meaning from symbols. It is possible, although beyond the scope of this chapter, to consider the semantics of paraverbal symbol systems such as body movements, sign language, visual images, films, architecture, and so on. Here we concentrate only on natural language and the various aspects of discourse. If semantics is generally concerned with meaning, then the most essential operating principle of semantics is interpretation. When I speak, a hearer begins the process of creating meaning by "interpreting" what I say. He or she does something like "assign meaning X to word Y," or "utterance U counts as expression Z." So words, clauses, sentences, and sound groups of various types are the subject of interpretations. Interpretation of discourse is a matter of assigning meaning to the various textual expressions in a discourse. The interpretations depend almost entirely on contexts, motivations, goals, desires, obligations, abilities, and social relationships.

Sanders (1987) argued convincingly that the most basic problem to be solved in communication is to control how one is understood. Typically, communicators want to minimize unintended responses and maximize the possibilities of achieving their strategic purposes. To do this, they must formulate messages according to the principles and conventions of social behavior and to the requirements of the individual relationship. Interpretation is an unavoidable and inescapable cognitive response to a message. Strategic communication requires a speaker or writer to project interpretive consequences, and as one increases his or her skill at such interpretive projections, he or she becomes more communicatively competent. But even the most unplanned and spontaneous communication is dependent on interpretations of linguistic and social conventions that allow for inferences beyond given information.

A second fundamental principle of discourse, and one closely related to interpretation, is "functionality." Discourse is motivated by the relation of language to the environment and is, therefore, functional by definition. Emphasizing the functional nature of language is important because so much of the history of scholarship in language (see chaps. 1 and 2) is tied up in a structural perspective. Functional linguistics is a question of language use and draws on a long tradition in sociology and anthropology (Hymes, 1974). That discourse is functional means that it is less concerned with invariant structures of language and more concerned with the specification of speech acts or ways of speaking, the gamut of stylistic devices, variations in language use, cognitive processes involved in interpretation, strategic communication, and the social relationships that provide the contexts for communication.

CONVERSATION ANALYSIS

One of the most interesting variations of discourse analysis is called conversation analysis (CA). CA treats the interactions of everyday life as sensible and designed by language users to be sensible. When people communicate, they are performing action; that is, they are doing something that is meaningful, purposeful, and designed to accomplish something. Action has meaning and carries symbolic implications. For example, I could move one of my eyes rapidly because I have something caught in it. My eye movement would be an automatic biological response that was not actional. But what if my rapid eye movement was a wink? A wink is actional. If you looked at me and concluded that I was winking at you, then that carries meaning and implications. When someone speaks, they are not just making sounds— they are performing action. They want to accomplish something and get something done.

The history of CA is interesting because it was a response to two issues. First, CA has its roots in sociology. By tradition, sociology was primarily concerned with order and knowledge at the level of the society. Sociology is mostly concerned with broad social structures and processes that are assumed to be naturally a part of the social organization of humans. For example, all human societies develop differences among groups and assign status to these differences. Thus, we have the concept of social class or groups that are associated with certain qualities and are assigned a status on that basis. The class system is a typical sociological concept. It functions at the level of the society and is assumed to be a societal function that influences human consciousness and psychology. Other social phenomena are concepts like "the state," "ethnicity," and "power." Conversation analysts such as Goffman, followed by Garfinkel and Sacks, challenged this tradition by arguing that ordinary everyday life was a legitimate area of inquiry. The CA people argued that there really was no such thing as sociological reality. All social concepts like class could only really be demonstrated in the daily interactional routines of people. This led them to study ordinary interactions and conversations.

The second trend was a developing interest in language as something other than a representational system for the world. Scholars agreed that language created actions. Related to this was an interest in unearthing what was relevant and meaningful to the participants in an interaction. Rather than the researcher bringing his or her scholarly vocabulary to the situation (e.g., objectively defining someone as a member of a certain social class), conversation analysts are interested in what is relevant to the individuals in an interaction. They focus on how the participants in a communicative exchange use language and rules to stitch together a message that is responsive to a previous message, and constraining for a future one. The goal of CA is to take generalities about personalities or social structures and see how social actors make them manifest. There is a sense of order to everyday life and a CA approach to discourse seeks to reveal the rules of this order.

Let us consider an example in CA terms. The adjacency pair is one of the most basic units of conversation (see chap. 7). Very simply, it is two utterances by two different speakers that are adjacent to one another; in other words, one utterance follows the other. A question followed by an answer is the most typical adjacency pair. Sometimes speakers ask a question where they prefer a certain response. They ask either a direct question or make a suggestion indicating that they have a preference for the other person to do something. Conversation analysts show how the second utterance in the adjacency pair is structured very differently depending on whether it is the preferred one or the dispreferred one. This is called *recipient design* when utterances are designed for the specific participants and contexts (Sacks & Schegloff, 1979). Look at the examples in Examples 17 and 18 from Atkinson and Drew (1979) as reported in Mateosian (1993):

17. B: Uh if you'd care to come over and visit a little
       while this morning I'll give you a cup of coffee.
    A: hehh Well that's awfully sweet of you, I don't
       think I can make it this morning .hh uhm I'm
       running an ad in the paper and-and uh I have to
       stay near the phone.

18. A: Why don't you come up and see me some⌈times.
    B: ⌊I would like to

Whenever the respondent in the second utterance expresses the preferred response, the response is composed of certain characteristics, and the same is true of the dispreferred response. CA has shown that preferred responses are (a) linguistically simple, (b) uttered without delay, and (c) convey information directly. The response of B in Example 18 meets these criteria. The agreement with the preferred response is simple, direct, and begins even before A finishes. The dispreferred response in Example 17 exhibits the following characteristics: (a) it is delayed [hehh Well]; (b) it has an appreciation component [that's awfully sweet of you] that mitigates the rejection and lessens the intensity [I don't think I can make it this morning]; and (c) there is also a justification [I am running an ad in the paper]. Thus, there is a logic and an order to the social action. Speakers know that rejections can carry interpersonal consequences so they structure their statements to mitigate and justify what they are doing. The opposite is the case for preferred statements.

How CA Works

Pomerantz and Fehr (1997) explained the essential techniques of performing a conversation analysis. They state questions to ask and issues to consider in attempts to analyze interaction. Following is an abbreviated description of how to conduct a conversation analysis based on the recommendations of Pomerantz and Fehr. Even the CA experts vary their approaches, and there is no single correct way to perform an analysis. But the approach described here includes the most important principles. CA is related to pragmatics and discourse, so there are many examples of conversation structures and sequences in chapters 6 and 7. The example I refer to in Example 19 is from Schiffrin (1994, p. 243):

19. IVer: (a) So there were a lot of mills around here
in the old days.
    IVee: (b) There was.
    IVer: (c) wow.
    IVee: (d) But not no more. ⌈ Yeh. ⌉
    IVer: (e)   ⌊ What ⌋ happened to 'em?
Did they close down, or-
    IVee: (f) Well, yeh, they w- they moved away or
they moved to Can- some moved to Canada,
some moved down south.

1. Choose a Sequence. Conversation analysts begin by identifying a sequence of interaction that interests them. There are many reasons why you might be interested in a particular sequence, but it is important to look for a sequence and choose a beginning and end. Example 19 has interaction preceding and following it, but we locate the beginning according to where the action of interest takes place. The final utterance in (f) is where the participants stop responding to the action of interest and perhaps move to another topic.

A sequence of interaction is potentially a very rich source of information. You might be interested in the interaction of people you know or of a context that you want to study. There have been conversation analyses of courtrooms, friends, medical interviews, counseling sessions, psychiatric patients, and many other interactions. Example 19 is an interaction between an interviewer (IVer) and an interviewee (IVee). It begins with the introduction of a new topic in (a)—the fact that there used to be lots of mills around. The adverb "so" is a good clue that the conversation is about to take a new trajectory. "So" is a continuer that projects action into the future. It indicates that the general conversation is going to be continued but take a slightly new direction. The sequence finishes in (f) with the resolution of the content under consideration, which is "what happened to the mills."

2. Characterize the Actions. Conversation analysts are interested in "action." Remember that action is the function and purpose of the language in use. When people communicate, they are *doing* something. They are directing their own actions and the actions of others. They are arguing, criticizing, agreeing, questioning, answering, justifying, congratulating, inviting, greeting, and so on. The relation between language and the action that a communicator is performing is very complex. It is not easy to say specifically that *this* language performs *that* action. Understanding actions is really a matter of interpretation. You listen to another person and interpret what they are doing. Even though the relation between language and action is complicated, we often recognize what our fellow participants are doing because we are competent users of our language. We have learned to recognize the various games people play with language; that is, we know what tools people can use to communicate certain actions.

In CA, one characterizes the action taking place. There may be more than one way to characterize it, but the analyst does his or her best. A good way to do this is to go through each utterance and write down the action being performed. This will produce a sequence of interactions that have some interesting relations among them. An utterance and the action that it performs is not an isolated and self-contained action. It has followed earlier actions and will precede future ones. Identifying the relations among these is part of interaction and CA. Following is an example from lines (a) to (e) in Example 19:

IVer:	(a)	So there were a lot of mills around here in the old days.	IVer initiates a new topic. Posed as a knowing question
IVee:	(b)	There was.	IVee confirms
IVer:	(c)	Wow.	IVer expresses interested affirmation.
IVee:	(d)	But not no more. [Yeh.]	IVee extends topic with question of current status.
IVer:	(e)	[What] happened to 'em? Did they close down, or-	IVer requests elaboration with suggested answer.

There are many things in this sequence that can be explained and analyzed. The interviewer's control of the direction of the interaction; the nature of questioning and answering; how the conversation is coherent.

3. Consider How the Speakers Use Language to Construct the Action. How Does the Speaker Provide Understandings by Designing Messages for Recipients.

Speakers produce messages designed to perform certain actions and have certain impacts on receivers. They do not produce these messages at a high level of consciousness. They do not slowly calculate every word they produce. But that does not matter, because CA is not very interested in the decision-making processes of speakers. It is what speakers *do* that matters not the cognitive processes involved.

Conversation analysts choose a particular action and examine how it was formulated, organized, and delivered. They also think about the alternatives available. What other ways could the action have been produced and why were they not chosen on this occasion? Moreover, given the way an utterance is performed, what does this make available to the recipient? For example, if a man is interested in asking a woman for a date and says, "Are you busy this weekend?" then he provided the woman with a certain amount of information before she answers. The statement forecasts his intentions and she can say "yes" and avoid actually rejecting him. The man chose not to ask directly.

In a slightly more sophisticated analysis, Schiffrin (1994) analyzed Lines (a) and (b) of Example (19) as an example of the existential "there" in a type of question–answer sequence. The speaker in (a) does not organize his statement as a direct question using auxiliaries like "how," "what," and "where." He uses what is called the *existential there* as a first mention of a new topic. The "so" helps establish the subject matter of the utterance. The fact that Line (b) does not include the predicate about the mills but is elliptical (i.e., leaves out the content about the mills) is further evidence that the topic of the interaction is understood. The pronoun "they" acts as a future referent for "the mills." The ability to keep the interaction coherent and sensible is an important part of the analysis and discovery of how communicators organize and communicate action.

4. Consider How the Timing and Taking of Turns Provides for Understandings of Actions. CA is very interested in turn taking or the system of rules and expectations that governs how you switch from one speaker to another in a conversation. Each turn on the floor—an utterance by a speaker with a beginning and end—is constructed, performed, and then is part of coordination with the other speaker to transfer the turn. For example, if you are in a conversation and the other person says, "I am going to dinner do you want to come?" and is then quiet for a moment, you "know" that it is your turn to say something. The first speaker has in effect chosen you to speak by boldly directing a question at you. But in other cases, it is not so obvious. You have to look for what is called a *transition relevance place*; that is, a place where it is possible to make a transition from one speaker to the next. Some of the most important issues are the timing of a speaking turn, how the turn was obtained, and how the turn was terminated. Violating the unspoken rules of turn taking can cause confusion and frustration in a conversation. It can generate perceptions of rudeness as well as misunderstandings.

The IVer in Line (e) begins his turn before the IVee in Line (d) is quite finished and at the same time that the person in (d) says "yeh." The overlapping brackets in (d) and (e) for the words "Yeh" and "What" mean that they were spoken at the same time. The speaker in (e) latches on to the turn of the person in (d) and begins by providing no room for the person in (d) to continue, should he so desire. Starting one's turn at the right time and avoiding interruptions and latches can be a show of respect for the other person. If you have ever been on an international phone call where there was a slight delay in the voice transmission, causing the speakers to overlap each other's turns, you know how sensitive communicators are to the turn-taking system.

5. Consider How the Actions Implicate Roles, Identities, and Relationships. This is where you relate the language mechanisms and turn taking to the people and their actions. Questions here are asked about the rights and obligations of each member of the conversation. Was the communication appropriate to the roles and statuses of the people in the conversation? Can you find relations between micro-communication strategies and macro-issues in relationships, roles, and identities? In Example 19, we can see the role of the IVer who asks questions and directs the conversation. This is a simple enough conclusion, but for now, it illustrates the close relation between the specifics of language and the actions performed by people in a role. It is the controlling IVer who feels empowered enough to overlap the other person's turn in (e).

This chapter focused on pragmatic principles necessary to account for discourse. These include mental operations but more important, the intuitive judgments about communication, including the speaker's awareness of truth, context, appropriateness, and presuppositional knowledge. Communicators must make decisions about lexical options, and hearers must interpret these decisions on the basis of propositional content, speech acts, implicatures, and principles of conversation. The next two chapters describe the various ways that interaction is organized. They examine additional issues in pragmatics, discourse, and conversation.

Discourse and
Global Organization

In chapter 5, we discussed the problem of meaning. We know by now that the literal meaning of an utterance is only one factor in determining its full meaning. It is widely recognized that all utterances may have multiple meanings and that communicators use contextual and general background information to establish meaning. Linguists disagree, however, about whether or not such phenomena are the proper domain of linguistics. There is considerable debate about whether or not the theoretical issues related to pragmatics and discourse introduced in chapter 5 should be included in linguistic study or relegated to some other human science discipline.

But the debate is less important to the communication scholar because the relation to some essential issues is clearer. The communication student is interested in performance rather than competence, as the distinction is usually drawn. Pragmatics and presupposition are more important than entailment. The communication scholar is interested in how available linguistic, conversational, and psychological resources produce a message designed to achieve a goal. It is impossible to explain goal-oriented message behavior by referring only to the logical semantic properties of a sentence. Communication is dependent on two things: (a) A goal-oriented plan that offers overall control and is functionally related to local surface connections an structures (*global coherence*); and (b) relations between utterances, sentences, or propositions that are pairwise and structured as sequential continuations (*local coherence*). These are the essential issues in discourse-level semantics and chapters 6 and 7 are organized according to these two discourse-semantic properties. We turn now to more specific ideas about interpretation in discourse. Just as we want to know the meaning of words and phrases and how they are related, we also want to know how sentences, phrases, and utterances are related so as to form an entire sequence. The basic problem of coherence or global levels of organization is how to account for information that is assumed.

Sigman (1987) described the approaches to coherence and the organization of discourse that we address in chapters 6 and 7 as perspectives *from above* and *from below*. The from-above perspective on how communicative language coheres assumes that the organizational features that make discourse sensible exist on the level of the whole. Discourse is assumed to be responsive to a hierarchy and organizational pattern. So an utterance, or written statement, is coherent because it is compatible with some general communicative agenda, prior communicative history, or some overall organizational principle. The from-below perspective draws attention to microbehaviors and the way in which units of language are adherent to local and temporally bound discourse constraints. Analysis from below focuses on utterance-by-utterance constraints and the use of text-specific structures that are related or predictable from one another.

It is of course impossible to completely separate and identify coherence mechanisms that clearly and only represent one or the other perspective. However, the distinctions between from-above and from-below perspectives do allow a researcher to decide how he or she wants to approach a communicative event. The example of making a public speech offers a clearer picture of the distinction between the two approaches. If we study a public speech—or, for that matter, textbooks on how to give public speeches—we would see that a speech has an overall structure. It has an introduction, body, and conclusion, and these can be further divided into subcomponents and strategies such as "establish credibility," "testimonial argument," "summarize," and so on. If we listen to an actual speech, there will be from-below components comprised of language, phrases, and sequential relations (and paraverbal cues) that are related to the overall structure of the speech but not determinate of it. The structure from above brackets the lower level units and makes them sensible. But the units from below can be organized such that more general structure is inferred. In this chapter, we take up the problem of general knowledge schemes and how they are utilized to make sense of interaction. In chapter 7, we examine the various issues and mechanisms that constitute local coherence, "from below."

REPRESENTING ASSUMED KNOWLEDGE

How do we represent knowledge that is assumed but not visible? We commonly assume that sentences acquire meaning as a result of their internal lexical components and syntactic relations. But it is also true that the meaning of a sentence can depend on assumed knowledge and a sequence of sentences as a whole. It is important for a speaker or writer to discover a way to ensure that a listener or reader can establish these relations to ensure correct interpretation. So a discourse is not simply sentences but sentences (or phrase units) that are ordered according to some idea. If a discourse is to be meaningful, it must satisfy various conditions of coherence. Moreover, there is a relation between the surface characteristics of a discourse and coherence. These surface features of text—namely, lexical choices, syntactic structures, mood, tense, adverbial expressions, reference devices—are typically termed *cohesion* devices and are the subject of the next chapter. Although we separate "coherence" from "cohesion" for clarity and analytical purposes, the two are never really independent entities. Most authors agree that coherence is concerned with "connectedness" and some sort of macroproposition, and cohesion with textual devices.

Global coherence is a macrostructural organizational scheme (van Dijk, 1980). Many utterances and phrases cannot be defined in terms of local linguistic mechanisms. We assume, therefore, that meaning in a discourse is influenced to a large degree by more general organizing schemes that are not immediately apparent from the linguistic building blocks of a discourse. Van Dijk (1985) explained:

> Thus a macrostructure is a theoretical reconstruction of intuitive notions such as "topic" or "theme" of a discourse. It explains what is most relevant, important, or prominent in the semantic infernation of the discourse as a whole. At the same time, the macrostructure of a discourse defines its global coherence. Without such a global coherence, there would be no overall control upon the local connections and continuations. Sentences might be connected appropriately according to the given local coherence criteria, but the sequence would simply go astray without some constraint on what it should be about globally. (pp. 115–116)

The statements listed in Example 1 might be considered related but not globally coherent:

1. I had Chinese food for dinner last night.
   The restaurant is near my house.
   My house is near the city.
   Houses near the city are expensive.
   It is difficult to get a good mortgage.

Global coherence (from above) provides an overall unity and sense of order to a series of utterances. Sometimes texts provide explicit cues about global coherence in the forms of titles, thesis sentences, headlines, and the like.

The headline of a newspaper story provides an interpretative frame for the series of sentences that constitute the story.

Metaphors for Knowledge Processing

During the act of communication (speaking or reading), we are processing incoming language information and also applying general knowledge that we have available to us in memory. *Bottom-up processing* is inductive; it is when language users compute the meanings of words by understanding the vocabulary and syntax of sentences or utterances they are exposed to. The meanings of words and the rules of syntax are the primary components of the computational formula for bottom-up processing. *Top-down processing* is deductive; it is based on the assumption that contextual information and previous knowledge are necessary to compute the meaning of a sentence.

Most of the work in these areas is from artificial intelligence (AI), which has blended the traditions of cognitive psychology with computer science. The primary goal of AI has been to teach computers to produce and recognize grammatical sentences. Traditional linguistics has been primarily concerned with grammatical renderings of sentences. And, of course, the computer is essentially a bottom-up processor. The goal of a computer, which has been taught to recognize grammatically correct sentences, would be to reject the sentences in Example 2. A computer that was processing from the bottom up would not be able to coordinate the vocabulary items because it could not make "sense" of the sentence structure:

2. A store are near the building. It finding confusing. People no longer knew well streets. I no knowing why.

Any AI computer program that tried to parse these "sentences" and rejected them as nonsense would be performing correctly. And any human language processor would also have difficulty with Example 2. But the human language processor, unlike the machine, would search for meaning. If you were engaged in an actual conversation in which Example 2 was the manner in which the other person was speaking, you would work hard to interpret what the person was trying to say. In fact, if you go back and look at Example 2, you can probably untangle enough of the language to make a pretty good guess at what the person is trying to communicate. A human can make sense of these sentences because he or she is not only processing from the bottom up. It is true enough that we begin with words and use them as scaffolding on which to build meaning. But it is also true that humans use a top-down strategy that has expectations about what things mean and how ideas should relate to one another. The storehouse of information and knowledge that humans carry around with them makes for tremendous predictive power. Top-down processing begins with expectations, so that if information from actual linguistic output is either missing, flawed, or otherwise degraded, the human language processor can "fill in" what is necessary. That is why it is possible for most people to make some sense out of the passage in Example 2. Van Dijk (1988) explained how the headline of a news story serves to structure expectations about the story that follows the headline and thereby assists with interpretation and understanding.

Any speaker or writer can assume some information. If I mention to a friend that I "taught my Monday afternoon class today," I can assume that certain information is available to that person. I would not have to explain that the classroom had desks, students, lights, blackboards, and the like. My friend could safely assume that certain communicative activities took place, such as lecturing, discussion, questions, and answers. All of these things would be assumed without being mentioned. These things are organized as a package of stereotypical information in memory. It is assumed that this information is organized as a whole unit rather than as individual pieces of information that must be collected and assembled in some way. AI researchers treat understanding, which is semantically related to coherence, as dependent on memory. Understanding is a matter of taking what you know (stored in memory) and relating it to what you are trying to understand; it is placing what you do not know in the context of what you do know. Global coherence works in generally the same way. A framework of information is called up from memory and laid over a discourse so as to make relevant connections and explanations.

When explaining communication and understanding, we must deal with the paradox that people obviously understand language, but we have little adequate theory to explain how they do so. Moreover, we do not need elaborate tests and experiments to show that people understand that two expressions may refer to the same thing (e.g., the ball and "it"), or that humans can explain the reason why someone performs a certain action. Yet, it is quite difficult to explain exactly how these judgments are made. But AI practitioners have argued that if the computer can simulate language understanding, then we will have specified the process. The computer program is a metaphoric representation of language understanding. The literature in AI is one of the best ways to understand global coherence because it has made good use of linguistics, psychology, philosophy, and computers to form a synthesis—cognitive science.

Scripts. The concept of script developed by Schank and Abelson (1977) has probably had the greatest impact on how we think about representing knowledge and understanding. A *script* is a knowledge structure that depicts a typical sequence of events for a common situation. Scripts are used to describe common situations like "going to work" or "getting dressed in the morning." The most quoted example of a script is Schank and Abelson's description of a RESTAURANT script where the script includes activities such as going to the restaurant, ordering, eating, paying, and objects such as menus, utensils, waiters and waitresses, plates, food, and so on. Each script has objects, roles, and activities. Schank (1973) began by trying to describe meaning as a network of conceptual dependencies. It became clear in the early AI work that there was a difference between representing the meaning of sentences as opposed to the meaning of longer narrative texts. It was possible to program a computer to parse a sentence and generate plausible representations of meaning. But it was necessary to infer causal connections between events if the computer were going to adequately represent the meaning of a text. Because it is impossible to determine relations between all the events necessary to understand a text by using only the language of the text, it was necessary to infer the existence of memories, scripts, plans, and goals.

The concept of scripts and script-based coherence began by developing what was referred to in the previous paragraph as conceptual dependencies. Conceptual dependencies are a network of semantic concepts that include information not available from the actual spoken or written text. This network of semantic relations can be quite elaborate (see Schank, 1973), but we simplify the process here. The text in Example 3 is dependent on the assumptions in Example 3a for understanding:

3. David painted the wall with a roller.
3a. David applied paint to a surface by using his arm to transfer paint from the roller to the wall.

Sentence 3a includes some information that is not in Sentence 3 but is still part of our understanding of Sentence 3. By developing these often complex networks of conceptual dependencies, Schank was able to generate a conceptual version of understanding that cannot be accounted for by syntax and the lexicon alone.

Learning is part of global coherence. Scripts also contain expectations about what objects or events will be present. When we learn, we formulate and refine scripts and then use them in the future. A normal person would have no trouble understanding what should be in the X position in Example 4:

4. John ordered a steak.
   When it arrived he picked up his X to eat it.

The conceptual nature of our understanding means that X can take any number of realizations (*fork, silverware, knife and fork, cutlery, utensils*) and still be coherent. Schank and his associates stressed that understanding is expectation based. The language of a piece of text cues us to understand the text in a certain way as in the following example:

5a. David took my picture.

5b. It wasn't a very good one.

We know what it means to use a camera to snap a picture and not think that the picture was very flattering. If this text continued, we would expect it to continue in this vein. But if we encounter Sentence 5c, then our script for this text has been wrong and we will have to reconceptualize:

5c. But I didn't think he would steal it from my dresser.

Because scripts describe situations in standard sequences, they have a more dynamic character. It is easy to move between and among scripts. It is probably true that much confusion and "miscommunication" results from misapplied scripts. To "take a picture" can call up a script that is composed of cameras, posing, quality photographs, or it can mean "to steal."

A script is assumed to render a text coherent if it can answer certain questions and provide a summary. A teacher in a classroom would make the same assumptions about a student's knowledge of an assignment. If a student were asked to read a story and then summarize it and respond to questions, we would accept the student's correct responses as "understanding." The story in Example 6 can be "understood" by a computer. It was processed by a program called PAM (Wilensky, 1981) and is reproduced here as it appears in Schank and Burstein (1985, p. 148). Note how PAM analyzes the story in terms of character goals and the plans used to achieve these goals:

6. (UNDERSTAND STORY 1)

John needed money. He got a gun and walked into a liquor store. He told the owner he wanted some money. The owner gave John the money and John left.

WHO SHOULD TELL THE STORY? John

I needed to get some dough. So I got a gun and walked down to the liquor store. I told the shopkeeper that if he didn't let me have the money then I would shoot him. So he handed it over. Then I left.

Q: Why did John get a gun?

JOHN HAD A WEAPON WHICH ENABLED HIM TO ROB THE LIQUOR STORE.

Q: Why did John threaten the shopkeeper?

BECAUSE HE NEEDED TO GET SOME MONEY.

Q: What were the consequences of John threatening the shopkeeper?
THE SHOPKEEPER DIDN'T WANT TO GET HURT, SO HE GAVE JOHN THE
MONEY.

Although these answers seem quite simple, they are answers that cannot be
generated by analyzing the vocabulary and syntax alone. It is not stated
anywhere in the story, for example, that "the shopkeeper didn't want to get
hurt so he gave John the money," or that John "robbed the liquor store."
The computer used its general knowledge to draw these conclusions. This
is a reasonable theory of how we understand things and use global scripts
to make particular instances in a text cohere.

The most serious criticism of script theory is the same criticism of all
attempts to model the general world knowledge to which humans have
access. That is, you can easily end up in an infinite regress of conceptualizations. To really arrive at a complete conceptualization of Sentence 3, for
example, we would have to include everything involved in David's moving
the paint from the roller to the wall, including his muscles, body, thoughts,
and so forth. We would also have to represent all knowledge of rollers,
painting, David, and walls, including linguistic and stylistic conventions. On
the one hand, this criticism is serious because it is probably impossible to
account for all such background knowledge and stop an infinite regress.
On the other hand, the criticism is not so troublesome because script theory
is a *theoretical* model and, awesome as it may seem, we can and must
assume that all this knowledge is available for understanding. We do not
need to assume, however, that it is always activated. We can hypothesize
an unlimited number of cognitive scripts that language users need for understanding and are available for processing. But we can avoid the infinite
regress problem by assuming that only necessary portions of scripts are
activated.

A second criticism of script theory is the problem of idiosyncratic scripts
or scripts that are highly dependent on unique individual and social experiences. We all probably possess individual scripts that are central to our
personal lives.

Schema. The concept most related to scripts is schema. However, there
are some differences. Moreover, the research utilizing schema theory has
been applied to some different areas. Schemata are higher level data structures for representing concepts in memory (Rumelhart, 1980). They are the
basic memory structures for the interpretation of experience. The case of
racial prejudice is one interesting application of these principles. We can
imagine an individual whose ideas about members of an ethnic group are
so fixed that he or she is completely predisposed to interpreting the attributes
of a group in a particular way. But a more plausible use of schemata is that

they do not determine discourse but provide background assumptions that lead us to expect certain interpretations. Schemata are useful for explaining how language users *construct* meaning; that is, people do not simply recall messages but use a message in conjunction with their existing knowledge to build a mental representation. We can understand the role of schemata better through an example taken from van Dijk (1987, p. 271). The fragment in Example 7 is of a prejudiced man (M) speaking to an interviewer (I):

7. M: Yes, you see them once in a while, you know, and then you say hello, and that's it.

   I: And other experiences with others foreigners or so?

   M: Well, never have trouble with Turks and Moroccans, but with Surinamese are concerned, yes plenty of trouble, yes.

   I: Could you tell something about, a story or so, about your experiences?

   M: Story, yes I once walked on Nieuwendijk (shopping street in central Amsterdam) with my cousin, still a free man, and well, then came uhh let's see four Surinamese boys. Well, they said something, funny remarks and all that. I said something back, and all that. That's how. So those guys I don't like at all, of course. So. Well, nothing against Surinamese, because my mother is married to a Surinamese man, so, but those young ones among them, that is, yes bragging and fighting and all that. So.

   I: Anything more you can tell.

   M: Well, as far as I am concerned they can all fuck off, in that respect. Then the good ones must suffer for the bad ones, but I never have such good experiences with them.

   I: With other, with other foreigners or so, you don't have

   M: No, never any problems, no because (???). Those Surinamese, that may fuck off. When you see what is happening. Are married, they are married, they divorce, women takes from welfare, and he has no job, but is moonlighting. We have have experienced that ourselves, in K* (neighborhood in Amsterdam), with my mother's friend . . .

The first two utterances of M establish that he has generalized assumptions about ethnic groups. The interviewer has activated his schema about ethnic groups and foreigners. Moreover, it is apparent that the evaluation that dominates M's schema is negative because although the interviewer's first utterance (request for experiences with foreigners) is neutral, it triggers only negative experiences ("never have trouble with . . ."). The cognitive schema for prejudiced individuals are marked for negativity such that they are predisposed to process only negative information. Also, part of M's schematic structure includes negative stereotypes about foreigners and Surinamese (they are violent, they carry knives, no job, welfare, uncommitted to family) and these are told in stories. The telling of these stories is one way that the assumptions of the prejudiced schematic are reinforced and control how information is processed about minorities.

There is also an interaction between the negativity of the schemata and the narrative structure of the story. Typical narrative categories are: SETTING, ORIENTATION, COMPLICATION, RESOLUTION, EVALUATION, CONCLUSION. The man in the interview fills the narrative categories in the following way (see van Dijk, 1987, p. 276):

SETTING:	I once walked on Nieuwendijk with my cousin. My cousin is still a free man (i.e., not married).
ORIENTATION:	Four Surinamese boys came along. They made a funny (provocative?) remark. I said something (provocative?) back.
COMPLICATION:	We had a fight. (I was cut with a knife.)
RESOLUTION/ EVALUATION:	
CONCLUSION:	I do not like these Surinamese guys.

The resolution and evaluation categories are empty. In his study of prejudiced discourse, van Dijk (1987) found that resolution was absent in ethnic stories about 50% of the time. In a classic narrative structure, the complication (fight) would have some sort of resolution. But because negativity is guiding the schemata, the goal of the storyteller is to communicate negative information about an ethnic group. This is easier when the listener is not presented with a resolution but is allowed to conclude that the storyteller was the victim in the incident. The essence of the story is simple and minimal. It is designed to substantiate the most general negative macroproposition about the ethnic group, and the succinct manner in which it is told is a very effective way to generate a negative evaluation/conclusion.

Schema theories can serve some very practical purposes in pedagogy and understanding the reading and writing process. Understanding a written discourse of any type involves a variety of complex inferences. The goal of a skilled writer, for example, is to help the reader follow the written material. A reader tries to impose a structure on written discourse, and a writer tries to produce a passage that can be comprehended. Cognitive processing at the level of schema involves more complex and abstract knowledge than processing the lexical and syntactic relations in a text, because a reader must go beyond the text and make judgments about the author's intentions. Understanding is significantly enhanced if there is convergence between the structure of a text and the reader's familiarity with the structure. For example, if an author has written a fable and the reader is familiar with fables, then the story will be much easier to understand. This is because fables are constructed according to conventions. They are usually epigrammatic with animals, men, gods, and characters. The fable illustrates a moral and is usually explicitly stated at the end. If a reader does not have a schema to attach to the discourse, he or she will initiate a bottom-up strategy by attaching meaning to lexical and syntactic forms. But if a reader or listener can apply interpretive schemes to the text, then a top-down strategy will be used and he or she can begin to apply meaning to the propositions in the story. In the fable example, a reader can interpret events by relating the action of the characters to a more general lesson.

Language interpreters at the United Nations often report that they "interpret the man rather than the language." It is very difficult to simultaneously translate from one language to another, because the meaning of a word is not self-contained. It is dependent on other words or the general "scheme" of the subject matter. Many United Nations interpreters prefer to restrict the subject matter and the people they translate so they can get to know them better. In other words, translators improve their ability as they develop cognitive schema that help them interrelate their knowledge of a subject and a person's communication patterns with the text to be interpreted.

The importance of schema for interpretation is underscored by research on cultural differences in understanding that are attributable to schema differences. Cultures probably have different assumptions for their texts. Comprehension should suffer if a text varies from the conventional schema of the culture. One study (Kintsch & Greene, 1978) tested the comprehension of Americans who read stories based on European cultures and compared these results to stories based on Apache Indian culture. Even though the authors found differences, it was still difficult to conclude that there were cultural differences, because no direct comparisons were made. Tannen (1984) also noted interesting cultural differences in the application of schemes for interpretation. She showed Greeks and Americans a film about picking pears from a tree. The film had sound but no dialogue. Spoken and written stories were then elicited from the individuals representing the two cultures. Tannen found that Greeks told better stories organized around a central theme and had eliminated needless details. The Americans, on the other hand, were wordier and more jargonistic by employing cinema language ("soundtrack," "camera angle"). Moreover, Americans seemed to be interpreting on the basis of a set of expectations (schemes) about how they "should" respond as participants in an experiment. The Greeks were more conversational. The differences in culture resulted in attention to different aspects of the interaction that influenced topical focus and elaboration. The participants in the experiment were clearly using cultural schemas to respond to the film.

Interpretation involves the selection and application of multiple schemes and parts of schemes. Consider the following example:

8. David, who is a funny kid, was going to paint my house and asked if I liked Jackson Pollack.

Interpretation requires a scheme for "David," "funny," "paint (house paint)," "paint (fine art)," and "Jackson Pollack." It is necessary to activate all or part of these schemes and make decisions among endless numbers of interpretations. A human interpreter can control both stereotypical knowledge and unusual or strange interpretations. A system such as a computer, armed with interpretive schema, must understand the irony, contradictions, and humor in Sentence 8.

TOPICALITY

The term *topic* is important in the study of discourse. It is essential to notions of coherence and is perhaps the primary organizational principle of global coherence. Discourse topic has an intuitive appeal, because all language users can recognize how what they say or write is related to a general topic; topics organize language. Textbooks that offer advice on the process of writing and speaking spend lots of time on the notion of topic. Principles of organization, relevance, and comprehensibility in oral or written discourse are all fundamentally related to the topic of the discourse. It is probably impossible to be precise about the nature of topicality, or to assume that we can formally specify the relation between texts and topics, but the concept still has strong explanatory value.

The use of the term *topic* has a long history in linguistics, and this history stems from a fundamental notion in communication. The basic elements of any communication is that the communication is "about" something. There is a subject or topic. And when humans communicate they not only say something "about" something, but they comment on it. The *topic–comment* distinction is elemental to the nature of communication; all communications are a "comment" on a "topic." The goal of any written sentence is to communicate, so the linguistic tradition of writing has incorporated the topic–comment structure of speaking into the subject–predicate structure of writing. It is easy enough to see that the two are often the same, as in Example 9:

topic comment
9. Bill / hit the ball.
subject predicate

But we are not concerned with sentence topics and comments. For our purposes in discourse, topic is a more general notion about the theme or subject matter that is being talked or written about. And, more important, in discourse we are concerned with a speaker or writer's topic and not with the topic of a sentence. Discourse topicality is actually more complex than sentence topicality because it is more difficult to recognize, and it does more organizational work than the subject of a sentence.

The topic of a unified text is the issue of concern of speakers or writers. Most theorists assume that a single proposition reflects a discourse topic. This view is a little simple, but it was given credence in some early studies by Bransford and Johnson (1973). They conducted experiments to show that understanding a text depended on contextual and topical-level knowledge. Participants had trouble with passages like the one in Example 10, until they were given a topic for the text:

10. The procedure is actually quite simple. First you arrange things into different groups. Of course, one pile may be sufficient depending on how much there is to do. If you have to go somewhere else due to lack of facilities that is the next step, otherwise you are pretty well set. It is important not to overdo things. That is, it is better to do too few things at once than too many. In the short run this may not seem important but complications can easily arise. A mistake can be expensive as well. At first the whole procedure will seem complicated. Soon, however, it will become just another facet of life. It is difficult to foresee any end to the necessity for this talk in the immediate future, but then one never can tell. After the procedure is completed one arranges the material into different groups again. Then they can be put into their appropriate places. Eventually they will be used once more and the whole cycle will then have to be repeated. However, that is part of life. (Bransford & Johnson, 1973, p. 400)

Participants were better able to understand and remember aspects of this text when they were given a topic. If this text were titled "Washing the Clothes," it would make more sense. The various actions and activities can easily be related to the topic of the text. Reread Example 10 with "Washing the Clothes" in mind and see how easy it is to understand.

Topic Scheme

The concept of topic is attractive because it is a primary organizing principle for either oral or written communication. It is especially important to the discourse theorist because it organizes a collection of sentences or utterances into a coherent whole. The concept of topic is also a very practical means of distinguishing intelligible and coherent discourse from incoherent and even "disturbed" discourse. The following, taken from Johnston (1985, pp.

85–86), is an example of discourse that has topic maintenance and management as the primary skill problem associated with a disturbed child. It is a portion of a conversation between a mother and her 9-year-old son (Peter) who has been diagnosed as language disordered with an accompanying affective disturbance:

11. P: Sam XXX, meet some new people quiz. Sam—

    M: You met some new people?

    P: Yeah! Sam says, "Wake up you pumpernickel." [laugh]

    M: What?

    P: Jumps up and down, on the bed, and says, after he says, "Wake up." Sam says,
    "Bobby and Peter" and says, "You're acting dead, wake up."

    M: Oh.

    P: And says, "Do it again."

    M: Is Sam a little boy or a big boy?

    P: No, big teenager.

    M: Oh. He's a teenager. Does he live at the cottage?

    P: Yea, that's where he lives.

    M: I see. Is he a friend of Mike's?

    P: Mike's friend go home.

    M: I think I met him, Peter.
    You played ball with him, I think, one time when we left.
    Did he come in and wake you up?

    P: Uh, yes.

    M: Saying "Wake up, Peter."

    M: Boy, there's a lot of traffic today, I guess cause it's Friday. Peter, did you get the leaf that I sent you?

    P: Yes.

    M: Do you remember what color it was?

    P: I can't turn it on.

    M: Don't bother about it, it's all right. Peter, I'm so glad you're coming home today. I've been looking forward to seeing you today. I woke up this morning and I said, "Go get Peter."

    P: You no need these Froot Loops?

    M: Did I what?

    P: Rice Krispies and Froot Loops, one of these box is full of Rice Krispies and Froot Loops, one of these box is full of Kellogg's.

    M: What boxes?

P: Froot Loops and some Rice Krispies. There—one of these box is full of Kellogg's Rice Krispies and Kellogg's Froot Loops, one of these box is full of Kellogg's.

M: OK, where did you see the boxes you're telling me

P: Tucie. You know name is? It's a Tu-can bird. It's a Tucan bird.

Even a casual reading of the text suggests that Peter is having trouble maintaining the topic and, even more subtly, adjusting to topic shifts and alterations. Johnston categorized Example 11 for topic-maintenance properties and reported that 45% of Peter's turns fail to maintain the topic and 64% of those turns that can be categorized as topically relevant are responses to questions. The mother fails at each attempt to enlist Peter's cooperation at providing mutual reference so that she can track the changes in topical movement. In the first six turn sequences in Example 11, the mother is having trouble establishing the discourse topic and initiates efforts to clarify (her turns: "You met some people?" and "What"). Given Peter's failure to cooperate, she gives up and lowers her expectations for specificity. A number of theorists (e.g., Labov & Fanshel, 1977) have described disturbed and schizophrenic speakers in terms of various structural mechanisms in discourse (e.g., anaphora, lexical ties) and concluded that these features were unrelated to topic. The concept of topic is what defines the differences between coherent "normal" interaction and the language of disordered or clinical speakers.

One of the problems with the analysis of topic is how a topic is assigned to a discourse, how someone determines which is the correct topic determination. This problem is confounded by the fact that most conversations are composed of a variety of topics, but the individuals in these conversations can name and identify these topics with consistency. The conversation in Example 12 is an example of "small talk" (Schneider, 1988, pp. 324–325) and illustrates the variety and organization of topics even in simple settings:

12. A: You're here on holiday at the moment, are you?

  B: Yes, that's right.

  A: Good, super.

  B: Mhm.

  A: What country do you come from? Germany, or . . . ?

  B: Germany, yea, right.

  A: Yea.

  B: Mhm.

  A: Whereabouts in Germany? North? Northwest?

  B: Yes, that's right.

A: From the coast, are you?

B: Yes, I am.

A: Yeah.

B: I am from Hamburg, actually.

A: From Hamburg?

B: Yeah.

A: Very nice.

B: Mhm.

A: My brother used to work near Hamburg.

B: Oh did he?

A: Yea, I went over once or twice myself, to visit him.

B: Great! super!

A: Mhm. It's very nice countryside.

B: Yes, it is quite nice, I suppose.

A: Is this the first time you are here?

B: Yes, it is actually.

A: Great.

B: Yeah.

A: So where did you come in from today?

B: From Glasgow.

The conversation in Example 12 may be labeled SMALL TALK, but there are many additional topics that might also apply. It could be labeled GETTING TO KNOW SOMEONE, and there are many subtopics dealing with RESI-DENCE, LOCATION, HOME, FAMILY, and TRAVEL.

Both Schneider (1988) and Planalp and Tracy (1980) reported that lan guage users are aware of topics and competent at identifying topics and topic boundaries. Planalp and Tracy asked 60 participants to segment a conversation into various topics. One group used a transcript only and another group used videotapes and read transcripts. The participants were extremely reliable at segmenting the conversation into topics, and the video contributed little or nothing to their accuracy. A strong explanatory concept of topic must allow all reasonable expressions of a topic to be included in the judgment of "what a discourse is about." For that reason, I suggest the term *topic scheme* as an expression of how interactants recognize what is appropriate and "topical" in a discourse.

In 1932, Bartlett introduced the concept of "scheme" to describe the cognitive organization of events and experiences. Schank and Abelson (1977) elaborated on this concept and proposed that cognitive structures are avail-able for interpreting information. A scheme is a framework that contains information about stereotypical sequences and events. A topic scheme is an array of topics and subtopics that go together. It is an open-ended set of events and objects that are required to interpret what the speaker is talking about. So a genre of communication called SMALL TALK is composed of a set that includes topics such as RESIDENCE, LOCATION, HOME, FAMILY, WEATHER, and so forth. Whenever interactants recognize a topic, they *impose* the topic scheme on the text such that subtopics are identified whenever possible, and topics in the scheme but not in the text are assumed to be appropriate.

The topic scheme is also instrumental in determining conversational relevance. Grice's (1975) cooperative principle holds that participants in an interaction conform to certain principles, one of which is relevance. Participants in communication are obliged to be relevant in their contributions or they will suffer negative judgments about their communicative competence. It is the topic scheme that determines relevance. A communicator is relevant when his or her contribution to a discourse is topical. The most typical pattern is for each participant to extend or elaborate on a previous utterance as in Example 13:

13. A: Where do you want to go for dinner?

     B: Don't know, haven't thought about it.

     A: Do you want pizza, subs, what?

     B: A sub sandwich sounds good.

     A: How about South Whitney.

     B: Oh, they are too slow and they never get it right.

     A: Lena's then.

     B: Yea, good.

Speaking on a topic, and making each contribution relevant to the general topic, is a feature of everyday conversation.

Topic Management

We must not lose sight of the fact that conversation is dynamic. It is a process whereby participants integrate their presuppositional pools to negotiate topics and topic changes. During the course of almost any conversation, the topic will move from one subject to another and perhaps back again. Competent communicators must learn to recognize and manage the fluid nature of topic changes. We saw earlier that participants in conversation are quite proficient at locating topic changes (Planalp & Tracy, 1980). There are generally two tasks that communicators must accomplish in order to manage topicality during interaction. The first is that a speaker must influence the interpretation of an utterance, and indicate the main topic, by making some information prominent. The speaker must organize his or her conversational contribution such that one element or idea is foregrounded and taken as the point of departure. Second, interactants must recognize cues that signal topic shifts.

Focus and Foregrounding. Not everything uttered in a text is equally easy to refer to or focus on. When people are talking, some information is prominent and in the foreground of the interaction, and other information is in the background. A piece of information is *foregrounded* when it is established in the foreground of consciousness and other information remains in the background. Consider a passage used in a study by Tyler and Marslen-Wilson (1982):

14a. The little puppy trod on a wasp.
14b. The puppy was very upset.

The "puppy" is foregrounded in Example 14a and 14b. The second line of the passage makes the puppy the main theme of the exchange. The effect of foregrounding can be seen by what happens if we continue this passage as in Example 15:

15a. The little puppy trod on a wasp.
15b. The puppy was very upset.
15c. It started to buzz furiously.

Line 15c appears awkward because it is responsive to information that is not foregrounded. The topic of the text is the puppy, and if Line 15c had been uttered, there would have been momentary confusion as the participants shifted topic emphasis. But any theory of discourse and how participants comprehend text must explain how topics come in and out of the foreground. There are at least two ways this occurs.

First, there is a distinction between *explicit focus* and *implicit focus* (Sanford & Garrod, 1981). Information that is explicitly focused is clearly foregrounded by being mentioned in the text. These items are clear to all participants in the interaction and can usually be clearly referred to with a pronoun, as in Example 16:

16. The book was really very good. *It* was well written.

Comprehension in Example 16 is quite simple because "book" is foregrounded and the referent for the pronoun is clear. Implicit focus, on the other hand, is when the foregrounded information implies other information that is logical or assumed by the topic, but that information is not clearly stated. Therefore, participants can hear Example 17 and still easily comprehend and integrate the information in the text, because authorship of a book is implied and implicitly focused:

    17.   The book was really very good. The author is very skilled.

A second very important way that information is either foregrounded or backgrounded pertains to the way people use their knowledge about the world and its general patterns to interpret a text. The different entering assumptions and information that people bring with them to a piece of text is perhaps most responsible for either clarity or confusion. A very interesting study by Anderson, Garrod, and Sanford (1983) showed how people use their experiential knowledge about typical episodes to understand a text by foregrounding some information and backgrounding other information. An episode is an identifiable collection and sequence of behaviors that go together in some way. Participants in the Anderson et al. study read passages such as the following:

    18a. The children were all enjoying the birthday party.
    18b. There was an entertainer to amuse them.
    18c. No expense was spared to make the party a success.
    18d. One hour later energies flagged.
              or
      Five hours later energies flagged.

The theory is that experiential knowledge of typical episodes would predict that the party would still be in progress 1 hour later but probably over after 5 hours. And the children are the foregrounded information in Example 18. The text was continued with either Sentence 19 or 20:

    19.   Playing the games had exhausted them.
    20.   Organizing the games had exhausted him.

The continuation in Sentence 19 was easily read and interpreted, whether participants read the 1-hour or 5-hour Line 18d because Sentence 19 extends foregrounded information, and the children could be tired after either 1 hour or 5 hours. But the continuation in Line 20 makes a pronominal reference to information that is not foregrounded; that is, to the entertainer rather than the children. There was more confusion and difficulty in understanding Sentence 20 when it was read in the 1-hour experimental condition than in the 5-hour condition because of the assumption that the party was still in progress and the children are foregrounded. Continuation 20 was read more quickly and there was less of an interpretive problem in the 5-hour condition, because it was beyond the expected bounds of the birthday party episode. Participants processed the fact that 5 hours had passed, and with that information, the children slipped further into the background.

In this chapter, we illustrated the principle of global organization of discourse, with particular attention to the topic of discourse. The assumption underlying this chapter is that there is a connection between the assumed knowledge of global organizational principles and the content of the discourse. Global concepts can be viewed as an element of content. The topic of a discourse can be considered one of the most important and central elements of the discourse. It plays a major organizational role and is central to the consciousness of the discourse participants. The topic or gist of a communication is what people most remember, because the topic is a central organizing feature. A global approach is the general guiding principle of topicality as presented here. It is in the same tradition of AI and cognitive science, which suggest that a discourse is constructed on the basis of general structures and organizational frameworks. Any discourse is relevant to a particular theme or topic.

A *genre* is also a global organizational scheme. A genre is conceptually and empirically similar to topic. A genre, like a topical structure, is an absent totality that refers to a distinctive category of things, such as discourses (oral or written), behaviors, or experiences. Again, like a topic, genres are conventional but highly flexible. They are organizations or formal means that constitute frames of reference for communicative practice. A genre is even a higher abstraction than a topic. The genre "romance novel" has an organization theme and structure, even though the content of each novel is different. Although topics and genres play an important and interesting organizational role in a discourse, it remains quite difficult to precisely tie the specific content of language to the global scheme. Nevertheless, a global organizational level is the one most communicators operate with while communicating. In the next chapter, we consider local levels of organization.

CHAPTER SEVEN

Discourse and
Local Organization

In the last chapter, we were primarily concerned with the global coherence of a text. Global coherence is essentially a cognitive perspective where the goal is to identify a macrosemantic interpretation of a text. In van Dijk's (1985) terms, global coherence presupposes the existence of a general structure that is related to ideas such as topic, theme, gist, or goal of discourse. It concentrates on what is most central or prominent about a discourse and acts as an overall executive manager of language, acts, and sequences. Local organization, on the other hand, is concerned with the pragmatic relations among actual components of a text. At its rawest level, a text is an unbroken string of expressions—words, phrases, and speech acts. Local coherence is "from below" or "bottom up" and focuses on how meanings in a text are linked up to form and contribute to more general and complex meanings.

In this chapter, we explore how more microlevel structures contribute to the interpretive act. Interpretation can be of various kinds, but it is primarily concerned with assigning meaning of the type IF X then meaning Y. An X is usually a word or syntactic form and Y is the interpretation or meaning of the expression. The various types of contributions to local coherence and interpretation is the subject of this chapter. We begin this chapter with a brief description of Halliday and Hasan's (1976) classic work on cohesion, because it is the most comprehensive and formal treatment of local coherence and has become a standard reference. From there, we build up to broader types of meaning by examining speech acts or utterances where the hearer understands the intentions of the speaker. Finally, the chapter examines the exchange structure between two communicators and the various sequence mechanisms that organize communication at the local level.

COHESION

We begin by examining some of the formal features that are available to a speaker or writer to signal a hearer or reader about how a text is supposed to be organized and thereby interpreted. We pay particular attention to the reference system in discourse. Up until now, we used the term *text* in a general sense to refer to functional language use or, according to Brown and Yule (1983), "the verbal record of a communicative event" (p. 6). But a more specific idea of text is concerned with the internal language mechanisms that hold a text together and contribute to its sense of being a unified whole. That is, how parts of the text are interconnected according to principles of binding and connectivity that require an interpretation. A number of authors have worked to address these issues in local organization of discourse (e.g., de Beaugrande & Dressler, 1981), but by far the most complete, technical, and comprehensive treatment of the problem is that offered by Halliday and Hasan (1976).

Cohesion and Text

Halliday and Hasan (1976) were concerned with cohesion that "occurs where the INTERPRETATION of some element in the discourse is dependent on that of another" (p. 4). *Cohesion* has to do with relations among surface linguistic forms whereas *coherence* refers to more general organizational patterns that lend order to a discourse. The dependency relation is key to cohesion. When one element of a message presupposes another, and this other element cannot be understood without referring to what presupposes it, then a cohesive relation has been established. Another way to think about cohesion is as a tie between two linguistic forms that assists a text with its sense of wholeness as in Example 1:

  1. Bundle the papers with string. Then place them on the curb.

The relation between "them" and "papers" is a cohesive tie. The function of "them" is to refer to "papers," and the cohesive tie makes it possible to interpret the two sentences as related. The term "them" presupposes "papers" and makes no sense without that presupposition. These principles of cohesion are part of the language system. The possibilities for cohesive relations among linguistic features are built into the language system. All texts (oral or written) rely on cohesion for their own creation. A text becomes a whole unit when its elements cohere with each other. These relations are local because they are properties of the text as such and not of some larger structure. Cohesion creates the continuity between one part of a text and another. This continuity is not, however, the whole of a text because general themes and patterns of coherence (see chap. 6) are also responsible for texture. But this continuity is essential for the reader or hearer of a text to supply all the necessary information and assumptions that are required for interpretation. Halliday and Hasan identified five types of cohesion—reference, substitution, ellipsis, conjunction, and lexical cohesion—but paid particular attention to reference, substitution, and ellipsis. The descriptions and critique here are necessarily brief.

Reference. All texts have some elements that refer to something else for interpretation. These elements are not directly semantically interpreted but rely on reference to something else for semantic interpretation. The "them" in Example 1 is an example. There is a further distinction between endophoric and exophoric reference. *Endophoric* reference is when a cohesive tie relies on some element within the text for interpretation: When a tie must go to something back in the text it is called an *anaphoric reference*, and when it must wait for something forward in the text it is called a *cataphoric reference.* An anaphoric relation says "look backward in the text for an interpretation," and a cataphoric relation says "look forward." An *exophoric* reference instructs the listener to go to the context of the environment for interpretation and not to some other place in the text. These types of reference are illustrated in Example 2:

2a.   Exophoric reference: I'll have that [person pointing to a sandwich].
2b.   Endophoric reference:
       (i) Anaphoric: I'll take this sandwich. It looks tasty ["it" refers back to "sandwich"].
       (ii) Cataphoric: That looks good, the sandwich ["that" refers forward to "sandwich"].

The pronomial system in a language does much of the work of cohesive reference. Halliday and Hasan (1976) explained how the most prevalent types of referential ties are personal pronouns (e.g., "he," "she," "it," "they," "him," "her," "theirs," etc.) and demonstratives (e.g., "this," "that," "those," "these," "there," etc.). Another type of reference is comparative where a likeness is expressed between two things. Likeness is referential because a thing must be "like something." Expressions such as "same," "identical," "similar," "different," and a variety of adjectives and superlatives all express comparative relations of some sort. All of these types of cohesive references are endophoric in that they refer to internal semantic relations within the text.

Substitution. The difference between substitution and reference is that substitution is a difference in "wording rather than in meaning" (Halliday & Hasan, 1976, p. 88). It is important to underscore the fact that all distinctions in types of cohesion are not clear-cut. There are instances of cohesive ties that cannot be distinguished clearly as one type or another. This is sometimes the case when considering the differences between reference and substitution. Whereas reference is a distinction between semantic forms and meaning, substitution is a distinction between linguistic items. A substitution is a relation between two vocabulary items or a vocabulary item and a phrase. The cohesion in Example 1 lies in the semantic identity between "papers" and "them." Pronouns are markers that instruct one to look elsewhere for meaning. Substitution, on the other hand, implies a repetition of a particular vocabulary item. So in Examples 3 and 4:

3a. Nice tattoo.
3b. Thanks, I am thinkin' of getting a new one.
4a. Is he sick today.
4b. I think so.

one and *so* are substitutes; "one" substitutes for "tattoo," and "so" for *he is sick today*. Substitutes can literally take the place of what precedes them. Examples 3 and 4 point up two of the three types of substitutions discussed by Halliday and Hasan. In Example 3b, the substitution is nominal in that "one" is a noun substituting for a head noun ("tattoo"), and in Example 4b, the substitution is clausal because "so" presupposes the entire clause *he is sick today*. The third type of substitution is verbal, where the term operates at the head of a verb group as in Example 5. The "do" in Example 5b substitutes for the verbal clause *turn the soil today*:

5a. We need to turn the soil today.
5b. I have no time for that, and neither do you.

Ellipsis. A third form of cohesion is ellipsis where something is left unsaid. The reference that is necessary to make a text cohesive is missing but "understood," as in Examples 6 and 7:

6a. Do you like blue corn tortilla chips?
6b. Yea.
7. David hit the ball, and the ball me.

There is a "slot" in Example 6b that is left blank but presupposes the phrase *I like blue corn tortilla chips*. And the second clause in Example 7 can only be interpreted as the ball *hit* me. Ellipsis is not the fact that a speaker must apply information from his or her own background to interpret an utterance, because that is always true and is of marginal help when explaining cohesion. Rather, ellipsis is when there is a structural place that presupposes some item that provides necessary information. The space after "yea" in Example 6b is a structural slot that gets filled by a clause from the preceding utterance. This is the same as substitution, except that in substitution, a lexical item marks what is to be presupposed, and in ellipsis nothing is in the slot. Ellipsis can also be nominal, verbal, or clausal, as in Examples 8, 9, and 10, respectively:

8. The test will have essay questions and multiple-choice questions. The multiple choice are least important. (slot for *questions*)
9a. Where are you going?
9b. To class. (slot for *I am going*)
10a. Larry was on his way over but someone called and held him up.
10b. Who? (slot for *called and held him up*)

Conjunction. Conjunctive relations are the fourth type of grammatical cohesion discussed by Halliday and Hasan (1976). Conjunctive ties are not primarily instructions for where to look in a text for meaning; rather, they are expressive of semantic relations that are presupposed in the text. Reference, substitution, and ellipses are relatively straightforward because they are primarily directions for interpreting elements in the textual environment. An interpreter is told to either "refer back" to some element in the text (reference), "substitute" one lexical item for another (substitution), or "fill in" a blank slot with a noun, verb, or clause from somewhere else in the text (ellipses). Conjunctions, on the other hand, specify how information at one point in a text is related to what has preceded it. This relation is semantic rather than structural. So the word "later" in Example 11 is a conjunctive expression that achieves cohesion through the semantic relation of time succession. The time sequence is the only thing that relates the two events. Examples 12, 13, and 14 relate the two events through structural relations of various types:

11. Bob finished work. Later, he had a drink.
12. Bob had a drink after work.
13. After work Bob had a drink.
14. Bob followed work with a drink.

There are a number of common conjunctive elements, the simplest of which is "and." Others are "but," "yet," "so," and "then." These are simple adverbs or coordinating conjunctions. There are other compound adverbs (e.g., "furthermore," "nevertheless," "consequently") and prepositional phrases (e.g., "on the contrary," "as a result," "in spite of that," "in addition"), all of which are common conjunctives in the language system. These various conjunctive elements in the language system can be used to establish particular types of conjunctive relations. Halliday and Hasan (1976) described four particular types of conjunctives they called additive, adversative, causal, and temporal. An example of each is in Example 15:

15. I spent the entire night working on my class project.
    a. *And* it was really difficult. (additive)
    b. *Yet* I am not very tired. (adversative)
    c. *So* I am almost finished. (causal)
    d. *Then,* in the early morning, I fell asleep. (temporal)

Conjunctions depend on meanings or sentences and on the generalized types of relations that we recognize. An *additive* conjunctive relation annexes information to the propositional content of a sentence. Such a conjunction typically links information along a series of points in an effort to contribute to a main proposition. *Adversative* conjunctions communicate information that is contrary to expectations established by a previous piece of text. The expectations can result from the content of the text or from something in the speaker–hearer relationship. The *causal* conjunction communicates that some information or state is the result of the condition just prior to it. These too can be links along a series of points that support a main proposition. Finally, when two successive utterances or sentences are related by sequence of time, the conjunction is *temporal,* as in Example 15d. Temporal conjunctions express a subsequent occurrence that is not necessarily causal, additional, or counter to expectations.

Lexical Cohesion. The final type of cohesive relation discussed by Halliday and Hasan is lexical cohesion, which is when cohesion is achieved by vocabulary selection. Lexical cohesion is perhaps the most complicated because a particular linguistic item does not necessarily perform a cohesive function. A vocabulary item contributes to cohesion when it is synonymous or near synonymous with another vocabulary item or when one term has a superordinate relation with another, such as in Examples 16, 17, and 18, respectively:

16. The book was very important. It was a rare volume of poetry.
17. He saddled his horse and rode the great steed into battle.
18. Roger bought a new bat. He just loved baseball.

In Example 16, "book" and "volume" are synonymous. In Example 17, "horse" and "steed" are near synonymous. And in Example 18, "baseball" implies a more general class of objects that includes a "bat." Each of these are cohesive because one lexical item refers to another. Again, "bat," "volume," or "steed" are not cohesive unto themselves but stand in semantic relation (reiterate) to the vocabulary terms that precede them. These lexical devices allow for continuity of meaning and stylistic variation.

Cohesion and Communication

Halliday and Hasan's (1976) work with textual cohesion is significant because it offers close analysis of organizational levels beyond the sentence. The most impressive successes in the study of language have been in phonology, morphology, and syntax. But there is very little work that relates issues in textual cohesion to more social and strategic levels of human interaction. Communication, by its nature, occurs at a number of levels (e.g., cultural, institutional, functional), but a concern with message strategy and effectiveness is at the core of communication.

Communicators are typically not very reflective about the use of cohesive devices; references, conjunctions, and so on are not under a lot of conscious control by people. But research does indicate that cohesive devices vary systematically with constraints on their use (Murphy, 1985; Sag & Hankamer, 1984). Ellipsis and substitution, for example, are oriented more toward the immediate context of interaction and used to focus on information that is currently under consideration. It is easier for individuals to use devices such as ellipsis and substitution. Pronomial reference, on the other hand, requires more effort from the communicators. They are more difficult, because speakers must have a firmer sense of how the other person has been interpreting messages thus far, so that speakers can feel confident that they will be understood. This process requires the speaker to take the perspective of the other and subjectively calculate the level and specificity of understanding by the other person before the speaker can make a choice about language. Various cohesive devices are also affected by whether they refer to the internal structure of a speaker or to the utterances of a hearer (De Stefano, 1984). We can presume, perhaps, that communicators who are particularly adept at tying their own utterances to those of others might be responsible for more integrated, smooth, and coherent conversation than those communicators who concentrate on their own messages only.

Research by Villaume and Cegala (1988) offers one interesting application of these ideas. Villaume and Cegala reasoned that the nature of a speaker's interaction with an interlocutor can be understood in part by how they tie utterances. They argued that a communicator's interpretive processes are revealed by the cohesive devices that help interactants with the burden of establishing meaning. They reasoned that interactional involvement, the extent to which a speaker is sensitive to and participates in the flow of interaction, would be correlated with the patterned use of various cohesive devices. In their study, Villaume and Cegala (1988) found that dyads where both members had tested low on interaction involvement did rely more on interactive ellipsis and fewer within-utterance references. In other words, their linguistic ties to each other's utterances were not explicit but reliant on the other person "filling in" missing information. And low-involved participants tend not to assist with the interpretive burden of the other, as evidenced by a lack of within-utterance cohesive ties. Interestingly, when low-involved speakers are communicating with a high-involved partner, they elaborate their utterances and increase their use of within-utterance ties; that is, they adapt to the high-involved speakers. This finding demonstrates that patterned use of cohesive ties is sensitive to speaker characteristics.

A study by Ellis, Duran, and Kelly (1994) posed a direct test of the relation between good communicators and cohesion devices. They showed that these devices were sensitive to contexts and people. First, it was clear that competent communicators used more explicit ties: Their messages were clearer and easier to understand. Those who were less competent communicators assumed more; that is, they uttered more messages that did not have clear links and expected the listener to fill in more information. This left more room for error and ambiguity. Also, the more competent speakers used language that indicated engagement with the other speaker. More skilled communicators take the meaning of the other person into account and create a greater sense of immediacy between communicators. They produce more verbal embellishment, elaboration, and pronouns that connect one speaker to another. The study also found some gender differences. Female speakers used linguistic indices such as relational pronouns (e.g., "you"), which is certainly consistent with the assumption that women speak in an "other-oriented" voice and are more concerned with "connecting to the hearer."

It is important to draw one distinction more clearly than Halliday and Hasan (1976) did, and that is the distinction between semantic relations and the textual expression of those semantic relations. Halliday and Hasan overemphasized the textual constituents of cohesion when, in fact, few would deny that cohesion is the result of semantic relations within the text. Cohesion depends more on underlying meaning relations than on the elements of the verbal record. There are any number of examples of texts that are easy enough to interpret but display no specific cohesive devices, such as in Example 19:

19a. Please pass the salt.
19b. What a beautiful table.

In this example, and in many other situations, there is not an explicit tie between a and b. But most people will assume that this example is textual and that the sequences are sensible enough from some perspective to assume that b is related to a.

Another way to look at this issue is to ask whether or not formal cohesion ties will guarantee texture. How easy would it be for a language user who was confronted with a text to understand the text on the basis of formal cohesive ties only. One interesting test of this is to jumble the organizational pattern of a text, thereby offering no global coherence clues and losing the impact of known semantic relations, and testing how well a text can be understood. Consider the passage in Example 20:

20. [1] 124 was spiteful. [2] soon as two tiny hand prints appeared in the cake (that was it for Howard). [3] Full of a baby's venom. [4] Neither boy waited to see more; [5] soda crackers crumbled and strewn in a line next to the door-still. [6] The women in the house knew it and so did the children. [7] The grandmother, Baby Suggs, was dead, and the sons, Howard and Buglar, had run away by the time they were thirteen years old—as soon as merely looking in a mirror shattered it (that was the signal for Buglar). [8] another kettleful of chickpeas smoking in a heap on the floor; [9] For years each put up with the spite in his own way, but by 1873 Sethe and her daughter Denver were its only victims.

This passage is the opening paragraph from Toni Morrison's novel *Beloved*; we need to say little more about how cohesion will not necessarily produce a passage that is immediately identifiable as a text. Comparing this passage with the correct sequence (1, 3, 6, 9, 7, 2, 4, 8, 5) demonstrates how difficult, if not impossible, it is to capture the meaning of a passage using textual connections only. A reader will use some of the verbal devices in the passage but is more likely to construct a general scenario that fits the events. Example 1 in chapter 6 shows how a sequence of sentences can "appear" cohesive but is really inadequate. There is the assumption that contiguous sentences that display cohesive ties form a coherent text, but this assumption can be dangerous. There is research that indicates that meaning, other than the most blatant, escapes interpreters unless they have more general organizational schemes for a text. The meaning of Example 21 is clear enough even though there are no textual cohesion devices:

21. Arrive Thursday, Bradley, flight #371 American. Call if late.

A study by Ellis, Hamilton, and Aho (1983) asked participants to take a randomly ordered conversation and resequence the conversation in what they thought was the correct order. The conversation appears in Dialogue 22:

22. 1 A: Ah, I know what I wanted to tell you.
     2 B: What?

3 A: What are you doing Saturday night?

4 B: Going to dinner and then a show.

5 A: Well, what time do you get done because there is a party which you are invited to.

6 B: Another party, I got invited to Bill's party too.

7 A: Really, he didn't invite me.

8 B: I guess I shouldn't have said anything.

9 A: I talked to Bill the other day.

10 B: Well, I was going to go after the show.

11 A: Maybe I wasn't invited because he knows I was already going to a party.

12 B: Mmm. I believe . . .

13 A: It's Sara's party and it should be fun.

14 B: Yea, where's it at?

15 A: Somewhere over on MAC.

16 B: This side of Saginaw?

17 A: I am not sure. Pete's going to find out this afternoon.

18 B: Yea, well the thing is the show gets out pretty late and . . .

19 A: I'll see Pete this afternoon and then let you know exactly where it is.

20 B: Well, we'll see.

This was a case of a complete conversation that was clear and simple to understand for the two people involved in the conversation. The participants in the experiment, however, were confronted with nothing but the text and cohesive devices as cues for how to understand the text. The participants clearly had difficulty making much sense out of even this simple conversation. Except for a few contiguous pairs of utterances, they were not very successful at resequencing the conversation. Pairs 1 and 2, 3 and 4, 4 and 5, 6 and 7, and 7 and 8 were easily recognized by the participants. Sequence 1–2, for example, capitalizes on the power of ellipsis to signal contiguity between the two utterances. The "what?" in Utterance 2 is only sensible if it follows Utterance 1, and competent interpreters will use ellipsis to tie the utterance to the one preceding it. Simple adjacency pairs (discussed later) are also easily identifiable by participants because of a strong local organization (e.g., 3–4). They are the type of pair where one utterance creates a slot for a particular second utterance.

But except for some highly prescribed relations, explicit cohesive ties are only moderately successful in creating texture and a sense of full understanding about a discourse. The participants in Dialogue 22 are an important source of coherence in the text. In a sense, they bring necessary information that is outside the text and cannot be ascertained by a close line-by-line reading of the text. It is important, then, to distinguish between the formal verbal record of cohesion, as described by Halliday and Hasan (1976), and the underlying semantic relations that "tie" propositions in a text. Language users do *not* rely heavily on explicit cohesion for interpretation. Texts are determined by those taking part in the communication process. It is important to reiterate, however, that Halliday and Hasan were not concerned with online processing of the meaning of text. Rather, they were interested in detailing the linguistic devices in the grammatical system that are available to mark cohesion. And although these devices are not sufficient to establish meaning, this does not detract from the compelling and heuristic nature of Halliday and Hasan's work.

SPEECH ACTS

The formal ties available to a speaker or writer are important for the creation of coherent messages. But participants in communication are also performing some *action* (see chap. 5). If I say that "I promise to mow your lawn," I am using language in our interaction to perform action—the act of promising. The distinction between the propositional nature of an utterance and its functional nature is important. *Propositional structure* refers to the content, subject matter, or ideas of a communication. *The functional* or *actional structure* of an utterance is concerned with what the utterance *does*. The example just given functions as a *promise*, and its propositional content involves *mowing a lawn* as opposed to a promise to do something else.

The British philosopher J. L. Austin (1962) was the first to make very explicit the different functions of language. He showed how many utterances are not just statements about some information but are actions. If, in the appropriate context, a speaker says something like:

23. I'll *bet* you $5 on the Bulls game tonight; or,
24. I *promise* to mow your lawn; or,
25. I *apologize* for what I said yesterday,

then the speaker is doing more than making statements about betting, promising, or apologizing. He or she *is* betting, promising, or apologizing. The utterance of these acts constitutes their performance. Each of the three examples is composed of sounds with conventional vocabulary and syntax; and each refers to some idea or subject matter. But each is also, as described by Austin, an *illocutionary* act that produces an effect on the hearer; each makes the speaker's intentions known. Another way to understand the illocutionary force of the utterance is to imagine each uttered in isolation. A speaker could utter any of the examples while alone, but they would have no effect and produce no action. But in the context of another person, each of the examples has a strong influence on the listener.

Speech acts begin to play an important role in communication and local coherence in a variety of ways. One way is by the choices that a hearer has when responding to an act. A friend of mine might say:

26. You should buy cattle futures.

I might respond with:

27. I don't think that would be a good investment.

The response in Example 27 would refer to the content of Example 26. If I interpret 26 as a statement, then it is subject to matters of truth or falsity. The anaphoric *that* refers to the content of the utterance. We could imagine the discourse continuing as a discussion about investment opportunities and strategies. But rather than the response in Example 27, what if I said:

28. You are always giving me advice.

Then I am responding to the speech act performed (advice) and not to the propositional content. Now, we might imagine the conversation evolving into an argument about our relationship. So speech acts can relate to textual cohesion by the way participants in communication refer to utterances.

An utterance is at one level *locutionary*, which means that it is made up of sounds with sense and reference. Traditional linguistics has been predominantly concerned with this level of analysis. Second, utterances have *illocutionary* force as described earlier. This is when a hearer understands the intent of an utterance and recognizes what the speaker is trying to accomplish. The third level is the *perlocutionary* act or the effect that an utterance has on a hearer. This has been the traditional domain of rhetoric.

Identifying Speech Acts

If speakers were always explicit about what they were doing, in the sense that they were clear about the illocutionary force of their utterances, then speech act theory would offer the most powerful account of communication. But speakers are often unclear about what they are doing; they are typically indirect, multifunctional, and vague about the purpose of their utterance. A speaker's utterance does not always have a clear indicator of what its function is, and even the use of a simple performative verb does not guarantee the illocutionary force of an utterance. Most of Austin's (1962) examples of speech acts were from highly prescribed and ritualistic contexts. When the preacher says "I pronounce you husband and wife" or a defendant utters

"I plead guilty," these are clear cases where the function and inevitability of the utterance is clear. The illocutionary force of a speech act is easiest to identify in highly conventional contexts such as wedding ceremonies, courts of law, and games.

But what about all the other cases where the purpose and context of an utterance are less clear? Most scholars have worked to classify illocutionary acts in terms of the recognizable intent of the speaker. This recognizable intent is an effectiveness criterion because illocutionary force is achieved when the hearer recognizes what the speaker intended to say or do. The hearer does not have to understand, agree with, or be affected by the utterance; the hearer must simply understand the speaker's purpose in uttering X.

There is still difficulty with the relation between utterances (actual language use) and the actions these utterances are supposed to perform. In other words, it is still possible to misassign a speech act or experience confusion about what function it is performing. When we are engaged in normal conversation, we must use the local lexical and syntactical forms to assign meaning to an utterance and, unfortunately, there is no way to map the language of an utterance onto specific speech act functions. Searle (1969) worked to specify as completely as possible the criteria involved in identifying a speech act and the situation in which that act "counts" as performing a function. He began by stating that normal communication conditions must occur; that is, the speaker and hearer must share a common language, both must be able to hear, and so on. From these basic assumptions, Searle extracted what he called constitutive rules for the performance of a particular speech act. The following is an example of the necessary conditions for the act of "warning":

Preparatory condition	Hearer has reasons to believe the event will occur and is not in the hearer's interest.
	It is not obvious to both speaker and hearer that event will occur.
Sincerity condition	Speaker believes the event will occur and is not in the hearer's best interest.
Essential condition	Counts as an undertaking to the effect that event is not in hearer's best interest.

A speaker might say, for example, "If you don't organize your expense receipts, then you will have trouble at tax time." This utterance would count as a warning because it meets the three conditions just stated. The hearer believes that he or she will have trouble at tax time and that this is undesirable. Both the speaker and hearer recognize that trouble at tax time is not obvious and can be avoided (preparatory condition). The speaker genuinely believes that trouble at tax time is not in the hearer's best interest (sincerity condition). And if trouble at tax time is not in the hearer's best interest, then the utterance counts as a warning (essential condition). The essential condition is most important because it is what distinguishes a "warning" from "advice." An event that is not in the hearer's interest is a warning, but if the event is in the hearer's interest, then the speech act counts as advice. If the speaker said "Organize your expense receipts and things will be easy at tax time," then an "easy tax time" is in the hearer's interest and the utterance would count as "advice."

Gazdar (1981) pointed out how the same utterance can perform more than one function. Statement 29 may be either a question or an inquiry:

29. Would you care if we went to Assagios for dinner?

Searle (1969) explained how statements such as the one just given have a literal meaning and form of expression and a nonliteral one, and that is why the utterance can perform more than one function. Levinson (1981) extended some of Gazdar's criticisms by faulting Searle and the principles of constitutive rules and claiming that speech act theory is too ad hoc and unable to explain how one act can perform more than one function. Levinson's example of "Would you like another drink?" can be either a question or an offer and the hearer's response ("yes" or "no") does not solve the problem. Levinson claimed that there is an indefinite number of possible act interpretations for certain utterances. He continued his criticism of speech act theory by questioning its reliance on speaker intentions that are not observable.

The criticisms of Gazdar (1981) and Levinson (1981) notwithstanding, hearers do interpret speech acts and recognize illocutionary force. Levinson's claim that speech act theory must yield a finite set of categories and a set of interpretive procedures is exaggerated. Speech act theory is essentially a pragmatic theory in that it must rely on assumed properties of contexts, metaphorical extension, interpersonal relations, and the sociology of language for interpretation. Language users correctly infer the illocutionary force of an utterance because they bring knowledge not only of language and grammatical mood but of speakers and hearers, personal relations, paraverbal behaviors that condition language, knowledge about communication patterns, relevant macrostructure propositions, and presuppositional knowledge. When all of these are brought to bear on an utterance, a hearer typically has little trouble working out the intent of the speaker (see Ellis, 1995).

Speech Acts as Interactive Accomplishments

Much of the data for speech act analysis is contrived. It is made up to demonstrate how certain principles apply. There is nothing wrong with these invented pieces of data, because they are examples of actual utterances performed by native speakers and thereby subject to analysis. But in practice, hearers often do not have a lot of help from the surface features of an utterance for interpreting illocutionary force. Moreover, speakers in "real" communication have the advantage of interaction history and pragmatic knowledge about the subject matter, context, and other person. A number of theorists have suggested that the interpretation of illocutionary force is not so easy as we move from one situation to another. We must ask whether the interpretation of a speech act from one context to another, or one relationship to another, is as unproblematic as Searle (1969) suggested. Is an "apology" or a piece of "advice" the same among government officials, families, friends, parental relationships, colleagues, and the like? Are they based on identical constitutive rules? Speech acts are a fundamental communication phenomenon, but their meaning and function are determined locally and perhaps not completely according to constitutive rules that are translatable across contexts. Edmondson (1981), for example, argued that speech act theory lacks a hearer orientation, or an orientation that is more communicative in nature by taking the perspective of the other. Actual language produced in communicative situations is hearer responsive rather than speaker responsive. A hearer is concerned with how a speaker's utterance is integrated into his or her own action, and the hearer's judgment about the function of a particular speech act is relationally dependent. The issue of whether or not speech act theory has slighted important cultural and situational constraints on language, and failed to account enough for interactively produced meaning, can be pursued from a number of perspectives, namely, interpersonal, cultural, pragmatic, and psychological.

One of the basic claims of speech act theory has been that constitutive rules of illocutionary acts are a semantic base underlying language and that different people rely on the same constitutive rules (Searle, 1969). This is open to some question, because it is possible to demonstrate that interpersonal relationships condition the interpretation of speech acts. In a quite comprehensive study of discourse in families, Kreckel (1981) argued that she has provided empirical evidence for the contention that constitutive rules vary according to the subcodes that they form. Kreckel used the term *subcode* to describe systems of meaning that are characteristic of highly specific communicative contexts. Groups of people who have very similar interaction histories and share much knowledge about one another and certain situations communicate, according to Kreckel, through subcodes. These codes are most typical in familial, ethnic, occupational, and specified cultural contexts. *Homodynamic subcodes* involve tendencies to choose the same forms of expressions and concepts and result in similar meaning through similar interaction experiences. *Heterodynamic subcodes* are when people acquire patterns of interaction in different contexts and through different communication media. In Kreckel's studies of family interaction, she assumed that family members would develop strong homodynamic subcodes. She had access to data from a film crew that lived with and recorded a family for 6 months (Kreckel, 1981, p. 5). Kreckel used this empirical data to examine two questions about illocutionary acts.

One question that can be asked is whether or not different language users use illocutionary acts according to the same rules. In one investigation, members of different families were asked to generate commonsense definitions of more than 100 speech acts. Each member of the different families stated what situations were relevant for an utterance to count as a warning, advice, and so on. Each family member discussed in detail what was meant by various illocutionary acts. This procedure allowed for comparisons within and between families as well as comparisons of subcode-specific rules with Searle's rules. Kreckel reported that comparisons of definitions for illocutionary acts showed powerful consistency within families and marked differences between families. For example, one comparison was for the illocutionary act of "warning." Searle (1969, p. 67) suggested that warnings do not include the necessity of taking evasive action, but Kreckel's data indicates that an attempt to get a hearer to take evasive action is an essential feature of "warning" as used by members of this particular homodynamic subcode. In another family, a warning was more associated with a speaker's attempt to get a hearer to do something than with an influence attempt.

A second issue concerns the degree of convergence between speakers and hearers as to what utterances correspond to what illocutionary acts. In other words, it is fair to ask whether or not speakers and hearers recognize various types of illocutionary acts when they hear them and whether they agree on their definition. Searle's classifications become problematic if speakers and hearers cannot consistently identify speech acts, especially because most speech acts are not typically uttered in the highly ritualized contexts that speech act theorists use as examples. Kreckel (1981) had her participants go through an elaborate procedure of classifying messages. She took a sample of interaction and had participants categorize various segments of the message into classes of communicative concepts such as "warning," "threatening," "asserting," "suggesting," and so on (Kreckel, 1981, pp. 131–137). Kreckel found that homodynamic subcode users (family members) had much higher classification agreement than those outside the code. The understanding of messages and their illocutionary force is greater among common code users than not, and this is especially true in communicative situations where there is considerable shared experience and understanding. Sharing a subcode even increases the level of understanding of messages that are designed for heterodynamic conditions such as public speeches and presentation. It appears that native speakers who share a history of experience and language use draw on their linguistic and extralinguistic knowledge to interpret various speech acts, and they do this according to "constitutive rules" that vary from the ideal grid of speech act theorists.

This debate can be extended by arguing and demonstrating that acts of speech are not asocial and translatable across cultural contexts. As I have suggested, speech act theorists are rightly concerned with communicative intentions but have described speech acts as the accomplishments of individuals who are not influenced by their relationships or local interaction practices. A cultural perspective on speech act theory holds that language is not a resource to represent the world (such that the individual can assert, promise, warn) but that words are relevant to relationships and how people come to understand the world. Rosaldo (1982) complemented Kreckel's work with her ethnolinguistic study of the Ilongots of the Northern Luzon in the Philippines. Rosaldo explained how speech acts in Searle's and Austin's work focuses on the inner nature of the speaker. Austin (1962) was concentrating on conventional acts in ritualized contexts such as marriage ceremonies and the like. When Searle elaborated on this and used the act of promising as an exemplar, he directed attention to the inner life of individuals and how a set of rules (constitutive) can logically transform the inner life of a speaker into a public statement of action. Searle forgot that promises are offered only in certain situations to certain kinds of people; that promises to or from a wife, colleague, neighbor, political figure, or child are different things indeed because meaning is not, according to our cultural stereotype, located only in people. Rather, meanings are shaped by culturally particular acts, beliefs, relationships, and practices.

The Ilongots employ verbal action that cannot be separated from issues in social order and ways of speaking. Rosaldo (1982) explained, for example, that Ilongots do not use "propositions" (e.g., assertions, statements, argument, claims) to state something true or false about the world. Although Ilongots have some similar speech acts (words to "explain," "tell," "advise"), they are typically used in the beginning of an utterance and are concerned with the formulation of relationships and the establishment of individual character. The Ilongots are less concerned with statements of fact than with who holds knowledge and the speaker's relationship to the holder of knowledge. The Ilongots use directives as do English speakers, but overt directives ("Go get the garbage") are "not considered as harsh or impolite" (p. 216). This is because directives have less to do with speaker wishes and demands and are more to do with affirming social relationships. Directives for the Ilongots are typically acknowledged, and rather than being characterized by a structured speaker prerogative, they are one pair part in an adjacency pair (Sacks, 1973). Directives are answered with agreements, acknowledgments, denials, and so forth. The power of directives rests not in their ability to match speakers' wants with a social act but in their place in the unfolding discourse between two individuals (Rosaldo, 1982, p. 217). Rosaldo's Ilongot data are an important attempt to modify, not reject, Searle's categorizations and explanations of speech acts by making them more sensitive to sociological and interactional constraints (see also Bach & Harnish, 1979; Labov & Fanshel, 1977).

Jacobs and Jackson (1983) explained how social actors use speech acts coherently, not because these acts are part of an established and predictable pattern of exchange, but because the particular speech acts in an interaction are locally defined ways to achieve communicative goals. Jacobs and Jackson's rational model of conversational coherence is reliant on a theory of practical reasoning constrained by locally defined ways of achieving goals.

Consider the indirect response in Example 34b:

30a. What time is it?

30b. Kelly's class just let out.

The reply in Example 30b is indirect and does not express what is called for. But it can be interpreted as sensible and coherent because it is the result of practical reasoning, a process that takes the shared knowledge of the speaker and hearer (the hour that Kelly's class lets out) and uses the cooperative principle to associate the utterance with the shared knowledge. Speech acts are not necessarily a function of structural features of an utterance and a context but the result of overall efforts to produce a rational conversation. The second response in Example 31 is a warning. The goal is to keep the speaker in 31a from going to Katy's house. The "warning" was produced interactively as a pragmatic response to the speaker's goal:

31a. I am going over to Katy's house.

31b. They haven't shoveled their walk yet.

SEQUENTIAL ANALYSIS AND SEQUENCES

Sequential analysis research recognizes that a current utterance in an interaction provides a communicative context for the interpretation of subsequent interaction. The best example is when one turn at talk projects or implies the next turn. Such organization at the local utterance-by-utterance level was termed *conditional relevance* by Schegloff (1972), and a conceptually related term is *sequential implicativeness* (Schegloff & Sacks, 1973). This form of interaction recognizes that some first action occasions a second, and this second action is understood as related to the first. If the second action does not occur, then its absence is an identifiable event. *The adjacency pair* is the strongest expression of conditional relevance, where the second part of a two-act exchange is literally defined by the first part. So a "question" creates a slot and an interpretative frame for an "answer"; "greetings" occasion "greetings"; and "offers" implicate "acceptances" or "rejections" (see later).

But virtually all utterances occur at some structural position in interaction. Although adjacency pairs are examples of conditional relevance and structure, *any* utterance can be made coherent by a prior utterance and establish a context for subsequent turns. Just as no word or sentence is fully interpretable in isolation, no utterance occurs outside the boundaries of a sequence. As we began to explore in the previous section, the illocutionary force of an utterance can be profitably understood according to how it functions in relation to a prior utterance. The analysis of sequences is an excellent entry into the highly context-bound nature of interaction-in-use. For our purposes here, we define an *exchange* as an initiation that has no restrictions on possibilities, where what follows is more predictable (see Stubbs, 1983). A *sequential exchange* can be considered a single propositional unit where the frame is established by the initiation (e.g., adjacency pair). The following is an attempt to be more precise about statements such as "utterances are in the first instance contextually understood by reference to their placement and participation within sequences of actions." I rely on some work in linguistics, discourse analysis, and communication to achieve increased precision. Some of these proposals are advancements and modifications of principles treated in Coulthard and Montgomery (1981), Stubbs (1983), and Coulthard (1985).

Form and Structure in Conversation

The tradition of linguistics, which we have alluded to quite often in this volume, has worked out issues in phonology and syntax fairly well. There are concepts in linguistics of structure, well-formedness, and predictability that serve as criteria for evaluating the acceptability of words or sentences. In fact, many of these concepts have been established in considerable detail. Each of these criteria apply equally to discourse, which is the search for order beyond the level of the sentence, but as I demonstrate here there are some important variations and shortcomings. I also concentrate here on *sequential structure* as opposed to many other issues in the general analysis of discourse.

To understand the organizational role of sequential interaction in establishing local meaning, we must turn to a few basic concepts that characterize discourse sequence. The first is *structure*, or the constraints on linear sequence. There is structure in a sequence anytime one utterance presupposes or constrains the predictability of what can follow. A related concept borrowed from linguistics is *well-formedness*: The extent to which a sequence can be considered coherent or not. As I stated earlier, these concepts are fairly straightforward when applied to phonology or syntax but much more restricted when applied to utterance sequences. Discourse is surely not random (see Kellermann, 1991). And people, when confronted with random sentences or utterances, are able to recognize them as random. The principles that underlie this recognition are the subject of discourse analysis in general, and sequential structure in particular. There is the claim in discourse that "anything can follow anything," and therefore concepts such as structure and well-formedness are not applicable (Stubbs, 1983). But this conclusion is too hasty because it is possible to demonstrate the importance and well-formedness of sequential structure in discourse.

We can make judgments about the structure and well-formedness of discourse, but these judgments lie on a continuum. Just as the words of a sentence establish predictions about what will follow, so it is with discourse sequences. This is certainly true with respect to propositional content (see Kellermann, Broetzman, Lim, & Kitao, 1989). If a speaker says something about a topic, then it is highly predictable that what follows will be topical and relevant (Grice, 1975). The most fundamental structural rule in discourse is stated as follows. It is the rule of *contingency relevance.*

Contingency-relevance rule: Whenever two utterances, words, phrases, or sentences occur next to or contingent with one another, then hearers or readers will assume they are related. The first will be used as a discourse frame for the second.

This is true in all discourse and accounts for the humor of the exchange in Example 32:

32a. David played Brahms today.
32b. Yeah, who won?

The humor is appreciated through the realization that Example 32a frames the discourse as "musical performance," but 32b is a response based on the use of the word "play" for athletic competition. The contingency-relevance rule makes the "musical performance" interpretation preferred, but the humor is the result of a departure from this interpretive preference. It is easy enough to provide many other demonstrations of the structural and predictive power of the contingency relevance rules. Consider those situations where we hear only one person in a conversation (e.g., telephone, person in next room, etc.) and how well we are able to predict what the other person is saying.

Even though it is sometimes argued that anything can follow anything in human interaction and hence sequences are not very binding, the fact that we can recognize incoherence is evidence that coherence is preferred. Nevertheless, discourse structure is likely to be somewhat less deterministic because it is constructed by two different language users, which is not true of the linguistic system in general. One person can never absolutely determine what another person says. That is why discourse structure is most easily responsive to maxims of cooperation (Grice, 1975). Given that what B says will be interpreted within the framework of A's contribution, it is possible to talk about discourse structure. Sequential relations control much of the meaning in discourse. Sanders (1987) has shown that explaining the contribution of a communicator by reference to attitudes, personality, or knowledge of subject matter is secondary to other considerations. Structural relations control meaning in discourse by classifying certain utterances. It is possible to show that the syntax and semantics of a speaker's utterance are often insufficient to account for meaning, and the utterance's position in a sequence is more important. It would be difficult to retrieve the meaning of the utterance in Example 33 if it occurred in isolation:

33. The rare chair.

But if steaks were being served and a speaker had previously asked "where should I sit?" then the meaning of Utterance 33 would be clear, and the discourse structure controlled the meaning. Communication is by definition strategic and for this reason, the disposition to say something and the nature of the propositional content are secondary to (a) whether the utterance is relevant and sensible at a particular point in the unfolding interaction, and (b) which subsequent messages are possible if a contribution is made at a juncture (Sanders, 1987).

SEQUENCE MECHANISMS AND COMMUNICATION

We have examined some issues in sequential structure and concluded that the exchange is the basic structure of interaction. We now turn to some specific sequences that perform certain "work" in communication; that is, a series of elements of exchanges that, taken together, comprise a coherent and orderly series of messages, which have internal structure and are designed to perform some desired action in conversation. Some of these sequences elaborate on adjacency pair structure and others are designed to prevent or repair the negative social status that often accompanies violations of social rules. Other sequential aspects of communication discussed next are included to demonstrate the range of strategic choices available to communicators. Individuals often do not have much voluntary control over certain patterns of interaction, or are simply not very reflective about them (e.g., turn-taking), but the variety of sequences discussed below can be used to understand and improve communication. They can be used consciously to increase the likelihood of achieving some interactional goal, or bettering one's strategic position.

Turn-Taking. The most basic fact of oral communication is that speakers and hearers trade off the roles of speaking and listening, and they do it quite competently. In a classic article, Sacks, Schegloff, and Jefferson (1974) explained that the rule of one speaker at a time means that the communication system must adopt techniques for exchanging turns at talk. If two people are talking at once, then they begin to remedy the situation by having one yield the floor—even perhaps as a result of aggressive talking over by another—or, if the problem is silence, there is pressure to fill it. So communicators try to accomplish turns smoothly without silences or overlaps.

A speaker controls the turn-taking system by exercising certain types of influence over the next turn. One, the speaker can simply direct who speaks next by naming the next speaker. An introduction—*It's my pleasure to introduce Robert Bently*—is one way to name the next speaker or asking a question directly to someone—*What do you think Bill?* The second choice is to manipulate who will be the next speaker but not select the person. Making a statement that is topically relevant to only one person would be an example. And the third choice is to select no one and have other participants select themselves. Sacks et al. noted that these three options are responsive to individual utterances and that there is an ordering preference. If one speaker selects a next speaker and somehow that selection is interfered with, then the right of the selected speaker is preserved:

34. Bill: [to Tom] How'd you like the movie?
    Pete: Oh, I thought it was . . .
    Bill: I was talking to Tom.

An even more interesting aspect of the turn-taking sequence is how a listener knows that the speaker is finished and it is time for the listener to become a speaker. Sacks et al. explained that it is impossible to be absolutely sure that a speaker is finished because he or she can always continue, but there are points of possible completion. Learning how to use these possible completion points is part of developmental communication. Language users acquire the technical capacity to recognize completion points and begin a turn at talk. In one case, listeners can predict the ending of a phrase or utterance and complete it for the speaker:

35a. My friend Roger ⌈is a fine mus⌉ician
35b.   ⌊jerk   ⌋

Or, at the completion of a sentence, two speakers may begin simultaneously and produce overlap that must be remedied. In this case, the rule that the person who first began has the floor is sufficient remedy for the overlap.

In a series of studies, Duncan (1973, 1974) discovered that cues for speaker change can be grammatical, paralinguistic, or kinesic. A speaker provides a *turn signal* that indicates a completion point. He claimed that all smooth turn exchanges in his data were the results of turn uptakes that followed one of the cues listed here. All confusions and difficulties resulted when a speaker tried to capture a turn when no cues were displayed.

1. Intonation: The use of pitch level and termination.
2. Paralanguage: A drawl on the final syllable or the stressed syllable of the phonemic clause.
3. Body motion: Termination of a hand position or relaxation of a body position.
4. Terminal expression: The use of stereotypical expressions such as "ya know" which indicate the completion of an idea.
5. Paralanguage: A drop in pitch or loudness in conjunction with a terminal expression.
6. Syntax: The completion of a grammatical clause involving a subject and predicate combination.

These rules change for different communication exchange systems. Conversation is the most common exchange system, and it uses a rule structure where the turns are allocated as described above. But debates, court proceedings, and discussion groups often alter the rules, especially debates and court proceedings where turns are pre-allocated; who speaks when is not decided on a moment-by-moment basis as is casual conversation, but is predetermined by an individual or the rules of a procedure. Pre-allocated exchange systems have the advantage of no interruptions and agreement on who has the right to speak. The turns on the floor are typically longer because of prepared and pre-arranged messages, and because there is little pressure on others to speak, which is not true of conversation.

Initiations. Although language users develop technical competence at turn-taking, they also learn many other discourse sequences. The two most typical sequences in an interaction, which all communicators must master, is how to initiate and close a conversation. There are probably three basic behaviors common to conversation initiation. Schiffrin (1977) described these as *recognition*, where two people first realize who it is they are talking to and categorize them in some way. They recognize each other as "friends," or "old acquaintances," or "colleagues," and so on. They also use this introductory moment to apply biographical information that distinguishes the person from others. Following this immediate cognitive recognition, there are *identification displays* where each employs certain behavior cues that indicate recognitions. A smile, arm wave, or widened eyes are typical examples. These identification displays are behavioral but still function as recognition symbols for the other person. Finally, there is *social recognition* that involves actual communication. These are greetings, exchanges, and references to previous interactions, all of which escalate the sense of involvement with the other person. Schiffrin used these opening sequences as prototypical and able to explain the consequences of various departures. If one person deletes one of the sequences, then this can create an embarrassing moment or a snub. Person A might display identification cues but if Person B ignores them, the initiation process has been fractured and Person A will take offense.

A related concept to conversation initiation is Nofsinger's (1975) *demand ticket*. This is a verbal device that forces a speaker to have the floor. It is used when the initial opening sequence has been performed or compressed. The demand ticket is almost coercive in its power to obligate someone to speak. It is not necessarily a way to initiate a topic as much as it is a way to get the floor. The first utterance by A in Example 36 is a demand ticket, because it forces B to grant A the floor and attend to A's message:

36. A: Guess what?
    B: What?
    A: Last night Judy . . .

Nofsinger posited what he called a *pertinence maxim* that is related to a Gricean relevance maxim in that it states speakers should not say what is "pointless or spurious." The speaker should be relevant and consider their contribution important. The demand ticket works because hearers assume that a speaker who utters a demand ticket will not violate the maxim. The data reported by Ellis et al. (1983) in Example 22 included a demand ticket in the first utterance of Example 22. The participants in the experiment were significantly likely to pair the first two utterances in that example, because the demand ticket is highly recognizable and obligatory.

Telephone conversations are an example of variations on the initiation sequence. Schegloff (1968) stated that a person may say "hello" when he or she answers the phone, but this is an answer to a summons. It is not a greeting or any form of social recognition. Given that now a channel of communication is open, there is often a greeting that begins the conversation, assuming that the caller is talking to the preferred person. But answering the telephone is analogous to a second-pair part of an adjacency pair—*sum-*

mons–answer. Yet with the telephone, a complete summons–answer exchange only results when the subject matter of the initiation is broached. No genuine phone conversation looks like Exchange 37, and movies or mystery books that capitalize on patterns such as those in Example 37 do so because they realize the power of such a deviation:

    37. Ring-ring   Summons
         Hello   Answer
         (silence)

Hopper (1989) wrote about an interesting variation of an initiation that has become more relevant because of the advent of certain new technologies. Hopper's analysis is an interesting extension of Schegloff's (1968) work on initiations because Hopper described a type of initiation that can take place any time during an ongoing conversation. Telephone technology now offers subscriptions to "call-waiting" such that if one subscribes, it makes a particular situation possible: At any time during a phone conversation, a "beep" on the subscriber's phone will indicate that some unknown caller is seeking access to your line. To take the unknown call, the subscriber must momentarily terminate the present conversation and initiate the new one. The beep serves as a demand ticket summoning the subscriber to respond. The beep serves the same function as a telephone ring (summons) with the subscriber answering. The summons–answer structure is maintained during this unique communicative context as is the recognition sequence, exchange of greetings, and initial inquires. But after the initial inquiry, the subscriber reports that he or she is on the other line and then Hopper explained the various trajectories that are available in this context. The following sequence is prototypical:

    38. Partner: And you know that . . .
        SUMMONS: Beep
        Subscriber: Hang on I have a call on the other line
        Partner: Okay
        (switches lines)
        Subscriber: Hello
        Caller: Bill
        Subscriber: Yeah
        Caller: Diane
        Subscriber: Oh, hi
        Caller: How are ya
        Subscriber: Fine, hey I am on the other line
        Caller: Oh

The initiation sequence is the same up to when the caller says "How are ya." Rather than responding to this initial inquiry, the subscriber states the call-waiting problem. The terminal "oh" from the caller signifies a transformation in the situation (Heritage, 1984). Even with the unique communication opportunities presented by new technologies, verbal initiations are built by language users on the scaffolding of conventional sequences.

Terminations.   Interactants are also able to produce sequences that close or terminate a conversation. When finishing a conversation, there are three functions that the verbal and nonverbal communication must fulfill. The first is to indicate that the interaction is coming to an end and that contact between the two people will cease. This can be accomplished by a statement of appreciation such as "Well, I've enjoyed this" and nonverbal behaviors that signal decreased access, such as a backward or leaning orientation. The second function is to state a basis or opportunity for future contact. Eye contact and some statement such as "See you later" are adequate for this function. Summarizing and restating what the encounter has meant is the third function. Some of these processes are altered according to how well the interactants know one another; however, their basic functions remain unchanged. Partners who are less acquainted and have more status differential are less likely to reinforce one another. And low status members of dyads say less during the termination process. In dyads where the individuals are acquainted, they are more likely to express concern for the welfare of the other.

The telephone has been a source of research for interaction terminations as well as initiations. Schegloff and Sacks (1973) suggested that the first thing to accomplish when terminating a phone conversation is to indicate that there is nothing more to say. Terms like "So:oo" and "Well" signal the end of the topic and declining interest in continuing the conversation. In an investigation by Clark and French (1981), they suggested the following sequence: First, the subject matter of the communication is terminated as the interactants signal the completion of the talk; next is leave taking, where both parties make statements about each other, the conversation, and future contact; finally, the parties say good-bye and the conversation is terminated.

Terminating an interaction is a cooperative activity. If the two parties are uncoordinated with respect to when to close an interaction, then the person who wanted to continue but was shut off will experience negative social and personal status. In conversation, both parties are expected to jointly and adroitly move toward termination. They must agree that all has been said and both are willing to discontinue. The use of terms such as "well" indicate the end of the conversation, and if there is an attempt to bring up an additional topic, then a subroutine must be initiated. Something like "Oh, one other thing" will return the parties to conversation.

Preface–Follow.   Earlier, we examined the various social and behavioral indicators that accompany the initiation of communicative contact. Another common sequence is the *preface–follow* that functions to introduce subject matter of some type. An individual preface is an utterance-initial statement that signals the parties in an interaction that certain propositional content will follow. There are many classes of utterance-initial preferences such as jokes ("Did you hear the one about . . . ," or "I heard a joke the other day . . ."), stories ("There is something I wanted to tell you"), or topic markers ("You mentioned yesterday that . . . ," or "Speaking of . . ."). Prefaces can also be individual acts, but they become part of a sequence when they are followed by a contingent utterance. When a speaker uses a particular marker such as "well," or "now," or "by the way" to indicate a topic shift or some change in the utterance-by-utterance coherence, they are signaling the hearer that what follows is a deviation from previous utterances.

Full presequences (Jefferson, 1972) express the most complete form and function of prefaces. *Presequences* such as the one in Example 39 are a sequence of speech acts where the interpretation is based on a sequence yet to come. The presequence serves as a preface for what will follow. Typically, the presequence is psychologically motivated so as to avoid the loss of face that might accompany a dispreferred response.

39. A: What are you doing this weekend?
    B: Nothing much, why?
    A: Do you want to go out?
    B: Yea, sure.

Presequences are prefatory in nature. Person A was able to establish that B was available to go out. If B had said "I am busy, why?" then A could have said "Oh, no reason, just wondering" and spared himself the loss of face and difficulty associated with a dispreferred response. Prefatory sequences are responsive to the preference for agreement. As we have seen, adjacency pairs have second-pair parts that are preferred (e.g., an answer is the preferred response to a question; acceptance is the preferred response to an invitation), but on occasion, dispreferred second-pair parts occur. Presequences and prefaces in general are a way to mitigate dispreferred second-pair parts.

Pre-requests work the same way. They provide a preface to a question that will take place later in the sequence. In the following dialogue, A requests information before asking for what he wants:

40. A: Do you sell backyard furniture?
    B: Yes.
    A: Do you have wicker chairs?

The pre-request saves the speaker from risking face. It is possible for A to go directly to his request for wicker chairs, but a "no" answer is dispreferred and can be avoided if A can determine the possibility of the store having the chairs.

Compliments are another sequence organized around preference. Pomerantz (1978) demonstrated how compliments and their responses can be explained within an adjacency pair framework where some responses to a compliment are preferred (acceptance agreement) and some are dispreferred (disagreement). The following exchange would be a prototypical compliment with a preferred response:

41. A: That was an excellent paper you wrote.
    B: Yes it was excellent.

But Pomerantz pointed out that there is another social constraint that conflicts with the preferred form of accepting a compliment: The social taboo against accepting self praise. Responses such as the one just stated by B are seldom encountered—if ever—and look unacceptable because they are not responsive to the constraint prohibiting self-praise. Actually, compliment sequences are organized according to a sensitivity to the competing demands of accepting compliments but avoiding self praise. Language users solve the problem of these competing injunctions by adopting one of four strategies. They can downgrade the compliment, qualify it, reassign credit, or return the compliment. Examples of each of these are in the following example:

42. B: Oh, it isn't really that good.   (downgraded)
    B: Yea, but it still needs work.   (qualified)
    B: It is only because of your help.   (reassigned credit)
    B: Your paper was excellent too.   (return)

Insertion Sequences. Most of the structures described so far have had one pair or pair part followed by another; it is also possible to embed a sequence where one pair occurs inside another. Schegloff (1972) referred to these as insertion sequences, where one or more pairs is inserted in the middle of another pair. Insertion sequences occur because the speaker who is responding to a first-pair part is unsure of something or requires additional information, so rather than uttering a second-pair part, the speaker begins an inserted sequence with a new first-pair part. For example, Dialogue 43 is a prototypical question–answer adjacency pair:

43. A: Are you going to the party Saturday night?
    B: Yes/No

but Dialogue 44 contains an insertion sequence where the answer to the question does not appear in Turn 2 but in Turn 4. The adjacency pair in

Example 43 is expanded to include another sequence that adds information before the answer is supplied:

44. A: Are you going to the party Saturday night?
    ⌈ B: Why do you ask?
    ⌊ A: I dunno, just thought it would be fun.
      B: Yes I am going/or No I am not going.

The bracketed B–A exchange is an adjacency pair within another. Schegloff explained that the first statement of A makes some answer conditionally relevant. And if B does not supply the second-pair part, then its absence is noticed in the same way as if there were no insertion sequence. The interaction is not "complete" until the second-pair part of the initial utterance is produced. Insertions can of course expand adjacency pairs indefinitely, bounded only by pragmatic limits.

CONCLUSION

Chapters 6 and 7 have concentrated on the central problem of using language communicatively and that is the problem of coherence. Global organization discussed in chapter 6 is principally a matter of the general cultural and social knowledge structures that make the language and ideas of a text sensible. Local organization discussed in this chapter focuses on the pragmatics of actual components of a text. These include the linguistic ties that are primarily responsible for cohesion; speech acts or the action performed by various types of utterances; and the typical structural and sequential mechanisms that perform much of the work of influencing the local interpretation of meaning.

   These two chapters form an important cornerstone in this volume because coherence, and how it is achieved, is fundamental to communication. It is impossible to separate issues in coherence and the orderly and meaningful ways that people connect ideas from communication. Moreover, the investigation of the specific techniques of coherence mirrors the systematic study of communication, because both are reliant on form and strategy; both depend on pragmatic and semantic relevance. I argued earlier in this chapter that Halliday and Hasan could be criticized for relying too heavily on explicit textual ties for cohesion, and that coherence was more determined by the shared knowledge that characterizes the communication process. Both coherence and communication rely on form—from subtle linguistic choices to sequential exchange structures—and strategy, or that communicators use language, patterns, and rules in a tactical manner to accomplish goals. This interplay between form and strategy, pragmatics and semantics, is what drives the communication process.

CHAPTER EIGHT

Sociolinguistics and Communication

The study of sociolinguistics is the study of language variation and social significance. It is the study of how members of a culture, society, or group use language for social purposes (communication) and what that language tells us about the person or group. This may sound like a broad topic, but there is a sense in which it is narrow. There are all sorts of theoretical perspectives and studies that have something to do with language and social life, but sociolinguistics proper is more narrowly conceived. It focuses more on the reliable correlations between features of a linguistic system and the typical categories used to describe groups and society. On the hypothetical business trip described here, all of the experiences illustrate various socio-linguistic relationships:

1. You meet someone at the airport who grew up in Milwaukee and when they want a drink of water, they ask, "Where's the *bubbler?*"

2. You check into a hotel in Boston and the doorman is inquiring as to whether or not you want to park your car by asking if "you want to *paahk* your *cah.*"

3. From Boston, you go to New York on business, and your business contact has a new idea, but he pronounces it *idear.*

4. Inside a cab, your African American cab driver notices some kids rapping on the street corner. The cab driver says, "*Dem dudes be doing day thang.*"

5. In Chicago, your last stop in this trip, you are given tickets to a Chicago Bulls basketball game. The guy in the seat next to you is rooting for the Bulls by saying, "*Duh Bulls!*"

6. On your way home, a lady sitting next to you in the airport comments on the odd *mauve* and *fuchsia* colors of the airport seating area.

THE SOCIOLINGUISTIC RELATIONSHIP

You may have barely noticed these characteristics of the various interactions, or at least they may have washed over you with little conscious thought on your part. But if you step back and engage in a degree of objectivity, you can make many inferences about the individuals in these conversations. You enter these exchanges with minimum knowledge and assumptions, but after only a few sentences, it is possible for you to have a great deal of information about the people with whom you have been speaking.

It will be useful to introduce the term *marker* at this point and explain how speech is a marker of social situations and information. Anytime a linguistic feature such as vocabulary, sounds, or syntax cues someone as to information about gender, geographical influences, social status, personal dispositions, group membership, and so forth, then that linguistic feature is functioning as a marker. A language marker is a sign, or an indicator, or an index that signals the interpreter concerning social, psychological, or biological characteristics of the user. The cab driver who uses the habitual "be" and substitutes a "d" sound for a "th" sound is using language that marks him as African American. The language is an indicator of the person's ethnic heritage and experiences with the American educational system as well as other sociological factors. These indicators or markers have correlations with various social categories. A correlation is a statistical relation that indicates a probable relation but not a perfect one. In other words, it is theoretically possible for a person who is not African American to use language in the manner just described but extremely unlikely. A marker specifies a relation among the three categories listed in Table 8.1.

A linguistic feature in Column A uses the information also part of the communicative situation in Column B to inform us about things in Column C. So, an African American might say "thang" for "thing," and this would be a phonological feature from Column A. This would be a marker of ethnicity in Column C. Moreover, you might use features of the context in Column B to draw certain interpretations. Another individual in the conversation might assume that such phonological expression is low status. If you were, for instance, an educated person from another ethnic heritage who believed that there was a "correct" and best way of speaking, then you might make negative judgments about someone who says "thang." On the other hand, the cab driver's language use might be high status in some contexts involving his peers.

TABLE 8.1
The Sociolinguistic Relationship

A *Linguistic Form*	B *Context*	C *Social Context*
Phonological	Situation	Social characteristics
Syntactic	Immediate goals	Status
Lexical	Meanings	Class
Paralinguistic	Background assumptions	Gender
Nonverbal	Language functions	Education
		Geographic region
		Ethnicity
		Etc.
		Personal characteristics

The relation between linguistic features and social categories may be of various types. A relation between Columns A and C may fall anywhere on a continuum from invariant to loosely probable. An invariant marker would be one where a linguistic feature is perfectly correlated with a social context. In Hebrew, for example, the second person pronoun "you" is marked for gender. Other relationships are not invariant but highly probable. If you hear someone say "idear" for "idea," then you can predict geographic influences (New York City in this case) with considerable confidence. The speech of the African American cab driver is very marked for ethnicity and not descriptive of anyone who has not had the cultural experiences of African Americans. Most markers, however, are more probabilistic. Their accuracy depends on the nature of the evidence and the communication contexts. A female is more likely to know the colors "mauve" and "fuchsia"—thus, those vocabulary items are marked for gender—but this is not a strong relation and is subject to change.

It is very important to recognize that the impact of a context is also more or less probabilistic. Some communication contexts are so rigid and ritualized that the language is just about invariant. During a marriage ceremony, the preacher will say, "Do you take this man (woman) to be your lawfully . . ." "I now pronounce you . . ." Various behaviors and interactions are highly expected. The situation requires a certain language and pattern of speech acts. Other communicative situations are very casual. There is considerable room for difference, creativity, imagination, and variations on a theme. Going out for an evening with friends would be a communicative activity with fewer constraints and obligations on the goals, roles, and language of the individual. This is not to say that we are ever completely free from the influences of the social world. Even the spontaneous and casual times with friends have speech markers and are subject to social forces that predict language use.

A third important quality of markers is that they mark more than one thing. The fellow in Sentence 5 who says "Duh Bulls" is using a phonetic expression that marks many things. The construction "duh" for "the" is a class marker, an education marker, and a regional marker. This sort of language use is associated with a lower level of education, lower standing on measures of the social class system in the United States, and is more identified with the Chicago area. It is always misleading and incomplete to concentrate on a single isolated marker without accounting for a system of variations. Most markers are social rather than individual. They are associated with the probability of certain experiences related to family background, ethnicity, occupation, and education. For this reason, it is better to think about communication "styles" rather than individual markers. Users of the Black English Vernacular (BEV), as in Sentence 4, employ an entire array of language features that co-occur.

It is possible to draw inferences of the several kinds. The categories listed next are both data from which to base observations and social-scientific categories from which to draw inferences. These include individual characteristics, language styles, social descriptors, cultural patterns, and sociological relationships.

Individual Characteristics

No one can escape the influences of their individual experiences in life. All of us are the product of family background, ethnicity, education, geography, social class, and related experiences. But when you communicate with someone, you do not know any of these things. You do not know, to use a modern cliché, "where the other person is coming from." Language is the most common and important information you have about others. Language is one of the most reliable indicators of another person's thoughts, influences, and identity. You use language as an indicator of the personal and *individual* qualities of someone. As mentioned earlier, most language markers are associated with social experiences that we share with others, but the linguistic feature can still mark our individuality. Our language use and communication patterns can give strong impressions of individual character and motivations. Marketing surveys, for example, are designed to reveal hints of personality that can be used later for product sales and development.

Human discourse is always a kind of individual and personal expression, a verbal art. But very little is written about this from a linguistic or communication theory perspective because it is considered too idiosyncratic and unique to contribute to general knowledge about language and communication. There is much popular psychology about the nature and presence of pure individuality, but it is a difficult concept to clarify linguistically. Truly idiosyncratic speakers have never emerged from research, probably because language is so fundamentally social. It is better to think about an individual's language use as a combination of influences resulting in an *idiolect*. An idiolect is a personal dialect that characterizes an individual, and many social factors contribute to the identifying features. We discuss idiolects more later.

Linguistic Style

A person's language style is a powerful marker of the participants in an interaction, their relationship, and the purpose of the conversation. There is no such thing as a best style as much as there is an appropriate style, and this depends on the identity of the speaker and the purpose of the interaction. A style fits situations. It relies on a variety of linguistic phenomena to organize itself into a coherent pattern of usage. Confusion, misunderstanding, ambiguity, and serious problems in meaning typically result from a mismatch between style, contexts, and expectations. A funeral does not allow the same range of styles as drinking with friends in a nightclub. There would be serious consequences for the image and social identity of the person who attended a funeral and communicated as if he or she were at a party.

Formality is one of the most important characteristics of conversations and relationships. It increases or decreases the nature of differences between people, and distinguishes among many everyday contexts of communication such as work, home, friends, and so on. Age, gender, and social position are all very relevant factors in determining formality. Language style is particularly relevant because it is what we use to determine and interpret formality. Informal language use is quick and syntactically elliptical, with many contractions and phonological blends and assimilations. For example, if you went into the office of someone you know very well and with whom you have a casual relationship, you might say something like "you aroun' here, man. I gotta see ya 'bout sumpin'." Formal language use is more structured, with highly articulated sounds, and uses vocabulary terms that indicate formality. In this case, you might go into someone's office with whom you had a formal relationship and say "Excuse me, I have an appointment with Mr. Ellis." Address terms such as "Mr.," "Dr.," "Professor," and "Father plus last name" (e.g., Mr. Ellis, Dr. Johnson) are markers of formality.

The essential difference for individuals between formal and informal language use is the amount of self-monitoring occurring when people speak. Formal communication is more planned and is the result of conscious thinking about what you are going to say. Informal or casual speech is more spontaneous. Communication theorists and sociolinguists are interested in both but probably slightly more interested in unmonitored casual speech.

Social Descriptors

Whenever we speak, we surely reveal some personal qualities but also an entire array of social characteristics. With no effort on our part, we engage in language use that betrays our social, intellectual, and material background. Our language is an emblem in the same way that an insignia of rank on a soldier's uniform marks his or her position in the social system. An interesting thing about language is that it is much more difficult to manipulate and consciously control. I could buy clothes or perhaps decorate my house in a manner that suggested greater social class standing than the truth would reveal, but not so for my language use. Social class imposes on us norms and expectations about behavior. Class is related to subelements of education, occupation, housing, friendship networks, and communication style, all of which are produced and reproduced by language.

Other major social factors are age, sex, and geographic region, all of which are discussed later. The relations between class, sex, age, and geographic region are enormously complex, but these factors are very important in modern industrial societies. Relations between language and class, for example, are distinguished by differences in (a) social mobility or the opportunity to move up and down the class ladder through education and access to economic capital, (b) differences between manual and nonmanual work, (c) community cohesion or how integrated an individual is into the local networks, and (d) gender. Sex roles are influenced by biology and how a society divides its expectations about men and women.

Cultural Patterns

The concept of "culture" is especially important in contemporary communication theory. Language and communication are culture laden. That is, they deeply reflect cultural patterns and influences. Many forms of linguistic variation are attributable to culture, both broad societal levels of culture (e.g., American culture, Western European culture) and more confined subcultures (e.g., African American culture, adolescent culture). In a sense, this is obviously true, because language is one element among others that makes up the concept of culture. A culture is a symbolic construction. It is composed of language, traditions, rituals, customs, and so forth, and culture is expressed in cuisine, clothing, dance, and so forth. Given that people are subject to the influences of their cultural environment, we would expect linguistic variation to be tied to the existence of cultures.

Communication problems such as ambiguity and misunderstanding are often the result of cultural differences. Language carries the ideas and meanings of a culture. The Aztecs had no word or understanding of the concept "Santa Claus." Why should they, when such a figure was nonexistent in their religion or culture? Americans have trouble adjusting to Eastern European shopkeepers who engage in little or no communication during a service exchange. Nonnative New Yorkers believe taxi drivers and others in New York are rude because of what Tannen (1987) described as the New York conversational style. They like to engage in lots of talk, much of which overlaps with what the other person is saying. The rules governing these sorts of interactions are often implicit and learned only through early so-cialization or having spent a long time in the culture.

Sociological Relationships

Language is also an element of the social structure. The mere act of speaking a particular language carries personal, political, and ideological implications. All languages and cultures have rules for what is called the *address system.* The address system is simply the terms and principles by which one member of a culture addresses another. Addressing me as "Mr. Ellis" implies a different relationship and context of communication than saying, "hey buddy." In Spanish, referring to the person with whom you are speaking with the second-person pronoun "tu" is much more informal than using "usted." Many languages have this distinction.

Many cultures are bilingual; that is, there are two (sometimes more) lan-guages that either have official standing, or so many people speak either of the two languages that both languages have political rights. To have political rights for a language means that education, publications, and government administration of internal affairs are all conducted in the protected language. Israel, for example, has two official languages (Hebrew and Arabic), both of which have guaranteed linguistic rights (Gold, 1989). But the reality of linguistic rights is always harsher than the laudable goal of guaranteeing them. It is possible to guarantee language rights in a territory but not always personally. Thus, the minority Arab in an all-Jewish suburb may have prob-lems conducting the business of life if he does not speak Hebrew, just as the Francophone in a small village in Newfoundland will probably not be able to use his language.

Even though languages coexist, they are never politically and sociologi-cally equal. One language is always preferred and considered to be of higher status or more desirable. It is important to know when to use one language over another. This type of inquiry and study is called the *sociology of lan-guage* rather than sociolinguistics. Both are concerned with the variations in personal, stylistic, and cultural aspects of language but have different purposes. The sociology of language focuses on the relation between lan-guage and society with the goal of understanding the structure of society. Sociolinguistics is more concerned with stylistic and situational differences as they relate to categories of social organization in a culture (e.g., class, gender, region, etc.).

LANGUAGE VARIETIES

In some of the earlier chapters, we treated language in a uniform way, as if all speakers shared the same language. Linguists have traditionally been interested in language universals and the features of language that are common to all humans. But our daily lives as language users exhibit great variety in language use. Next, we look at all the types of variation that have been investigated and all the main geographic and social influences. We begin with the root concept of the "standard" language and move to the various branches and twigs.

Standard Language

All languages approximate what is called "the standard." This is the nature of the language shared by everyone who uses it. The standard is what the culture considers the norm and the most "correct" way of speaking. Standard language can be understood by all speakers of the language, and it is most associated with the ways of speaking taught in the schools and sanctioned by official institutions of the culture. When someone asks about "the right way to speak" or the "correct use of the language," they are looking for an answer that reflects the standard, which is what the educated classes of the society consider to be the correct way of speaking. Standard English is what is written in the newspapers, published in books, and used by the national media. It is what we try to teach in schools and is captured best in written language rather than spoken. Written language is more uniform and subject to more prescriptions than spoken language, which is more casual and creative, with fewer penalties for rule violations. Grammar books and the dictionary are the best places to find the rules and principles of the standard language in a culture. If you look up the pronunciation of the word "car" in the dictionary, it will tell you to pronounce it "kär," not "caah" or some other regional pronunciation. The dictionary is giving what is considered the standard. It will also have the most standard definition and not all slang or specialized uses.

It is important to understand that what is considered standard is theoretical. That means that it is an abstraction to be achieved or to guide language use, but in actuality, no one speaks a perfect standard. Dialects, differences, and variations are all departures from the standard. As we have been saying, everyone is influenced by personal, psychological, and social factors that alter the way we speak. Trying to find a perfect model of a standard speaker would be like trying to find someone who was "the average person." We refer to average people all of the time and could even describe them statistically in terms of income, height, weight, intelligence, and opinions ad infinitum. But if you actually set out to find someone who was the perfect statistically average person, no one would qualify. Everyone is different in some small or large way. Thus, everyone has an accent. Everyone speaks a dialect or some variation on the standard theme, even if it is an educated dialect. Some people speak more extreme and nonstandard dialects than others, but they are dialects nonetheless.

In Great Britain, there is a way of speaking called the "received pronunciation" (RP), which is considered the standard. It is spoken by anyone with an education, and all the regional dialects are considered nonstandard to some degree. The United States is more diverse however, and there are more regional dialects that are accepted as educationally standard. One can speak in an educated southern or midwestern dialect. But eastern New England educated speech is considered especially high status and fine, probably because of its historical roots and connections to British RP. It is the language used to portray any media character who is supposed to be highly refined and educated. The character of Major Winchester on the television show *M*A*S*H* used this linguistic variety for great comic effect. If you watch many old movies, you can see how actors (male and female) were coached to mimic the style of eastern New England speech, even when the particular actor spoke with a different accent, because it was considered the most prestigious. But since World War II, there have been noticeable changes in dialects.

Dialects and Accents

Everyone speaks with an accent of some sort. Some speakers may have heavy or distinct accents, and others not, but everyone speaks with some sort of accent. Technically, an *accent* is regional phonological variation. It is how different people sound in various regions of a country. A dialect involves greater language variation. A *dialect* is variation in grammar and vocabulary in addition to sound variations. For example, if one person utters the sentence "John is a farmer" and another says the same thing except pronounces the word farmer as "fahmuh," then the difference is one of accent. But if one person says something like "You should not do that" and another says "Ya hadn't oughta do that," then this is a dialect difference because the variation is greater. The extent of dialect differences is a continuum. Some dialects are extremely different and others less so. Compare the first two lines from the 23rd Psalm in Example 7:

7. A. The Lord is my shepherd
    B. Big man watchem sheepy-sheep watchem me.

Line B is technically English but extremely different from Line A. It is part of a highly metaphorized Creole language that refers to "the big man who watches sheep and me" (e.g., God, who is my shepherd). The "watchem me" functions as the possessive pronoun "my." In some areas of Ireland and the United States (Pennsylvania in particular), there is a syntactic construction called the second-person plural pronoun. The word is "youse," as in the sentence, "Where youse goin' " said to a group of other people. This is a lower status working-class construction that reflects some interesting dialect issues.

Vocabulary differences are the most easily recognized. People from groups or regions use some words that are different from others, and these words mark you geographically. Someone from the northern part of the midwestern United States is more likely to say "paper bag" than "paper sack." A Midland dialect (mid Iowa and Nebraska) is more likely to say "bucket" than "pail." Sociolinguists, and those involved in the serious analysis of language, can draw maps that have lines in them across geographic areas. These lines are called *isoglosses* and represent the boundary between one linguistic area and another. When distinct accents, vocabulary, and syntax converge in a regional area, you have a geographic boundary that encompasses a *regional dialect.*

Regional dialects are universal. All nations and cultures have geographic regions where features of language vary. These regions and dialects are usually a source of judgments about status and certainly a source of humor. In the United States, Brooklyn accents and Southern accents can be understood as funny, whereas New England accents are considered serious. It is important to remember that regional dialects display a lot of variation. If you traveled from the East to the West in the United States, you would discover subtle changes and see that dialects were not highly differentiated. Your trip would take you through areas that were very distinct and rich in dialect purity, but as you moved along, those distinctions would slowly diminish until you entered another isogloss.

Regional dialects are less pure than they used to be because the world is a "smaller" place. In other words, there is more contact among people and more influences from outside of our living regions. Television, radio, mobility, and the easier availability of education have homogenizing effects on accents. Your accent would remain quite stable if you lived in a small community of people and rarely left the community. If you had very few influences from outside of your community, then you would have very few influences on how you spoke. Many speakers move easily across borders and become competent in different dialects. They become *bidialectal;* that is, they speak more than one dialect. In some sense, we all speak more than one dialect. We can speak the dialect of our neighborhood and the dialect of our professional world. Again, these are sometimes quite distinct and sometimes not.

When dialects are most different and have developed in certain ways, they typically fall into the category of being either a pidgin or a Creole language. A *pidgin* language is a simplified language that borrows vocabulary but develops its own syntax. Pidgins usually result from historic contact between two cultures using different languages, but they develop a dialect that allows the two cultures to engage in trade and regular communication. Pidgins have numerous irregularities and simplifications. Moreover, pidgin languages are purely functional. They are rarely written down and children do not learn them from their parents. Example 7 from the 23rd Psalm is an example of a pidgin. Example 8 is a Hawaiian pidgin (Bickerton, 1981, p. 13):

8. Samtaim gud rod get, samtaim, olsem ben get enguru get, no? enikain seim. Olsem hyuman laif, olsem.

The person in Example 8 is saying that "sometimes there is a good road, sometimes there, like, bends, corners, right? Everything is like that. Human life is just like that."

When a pidgin language becomes more accepted and standardized, when it becomes the native language of a generation of children, then it is called a *Creole*. A Creole is a home language and becomes the mother tongue of a group of people. Creole languages must do the everyday work of life so they develop more elaborated vocabulary and regularized syntax. West African Creoles are good examples. In the worst days of the American slave trade, African slaves were separated from anyone who spoke the same language to prevent insurrection. Therefore, pidgin languages were the only available means of communication. The African slaves combined elements of their own language with English to communicate with others. This language became creolized and was the primary dialect of many African slaves, and even though it has passed away in the United States, it still influences contemporary BEV.

It is important to remember that pidgins and Creoles are difficult to define, difficult to study, and always controversial. There are usually few written records of the language or the history that produced the language. Moreover, these languages are always belittled as ignorant corruptions of purer languages. As soon as Creole speakers are exposed to what is considered more prestigious forms of speaking (e.g., Standard English or British English), a process called *decreolization* begins. They begin to drift away from the Creole and toward the more prestigious language use, which means that the Creole begins to disappear. Still, pidgins and Creoles are fascinating laboratories from which to study how languages evolve, syntactic development, and attitudes towards languages, vocabulary processes, and historical influences on languages.

SOCIAL VARIETIES

Students of communication are typically interested in social varieties of language use. These issues are more concerned with how and why speakers use the language they do and make it easier for competent communicators to understand individuals and communicative situations. Social dialects reflect how language varieties correlate with age, class, education, gender, and other social measures.

No two language varieties are equal. One way of speaking is always considered different than another, and these differences carry either positive or negative connotations. Before examining the relation between language and social categories in more detail, it is necessary to draw attention to one issue in language use. This is the idea of prestige and stigmatization in language. One language or way of speaking is always considered of higher status than another, and some way of speaking is always considered stigmatized or less prestigious. Of course, the language of the powerful and standard institutions (e.g., schools and government) is always considered more prestigious, and the language of the less powerful and educated is stigmatized.

Prestige and stigmatization occur either "from below" or "from above." When a group drifts toward a new sound or vocabulary item and they are unconscious of it, this is a change from below (below consciousness level). The introduction of language change is from above when the change is consciously introduced by higher status groups. For example, change originates when there is some fluctuation in language use due to contact with a new group or some linguistic influence. If, rather than saying "arithmetic" you say "arith*a*metic," or you say "fil*u*m" rather than "film," then you are adding sounds to the middle of a word and taking part in from-below linguistic change. If this change stays within your social network and is not adopted by anyone else, it marks your social network and will be considered stigmatized. If this stigmatization is extreme, it will become a stereotype and highly descriptive of your group. This happens to African Americans and other minority groups. When schools and government institutions issue guidelines about standard or correct speech, they are initiating change from above. If a high-status group (e.g., professionals, journalists, scholars, and teachers) originate change, then it is more likely to become associated with prestige usage.

It is important to remember, however, that status is a relative term. All of us belong to various subgroups in society. These are groups formed on the basis of family, work, professional identification, and social alliances of various types. The unique forms of communication characteristic of these groups can carry a prestige of their own, even if the larger society discourages or stigmatizes these forms of communication. A positive value can be attached to these nonstandard forms of communication and language use such that they express important aspects of identity and group affiliation. When adolescent boys use slang and "bad" language, they are using language that is positively valued to them. Later in this chapter, we see that African Americans are regularly mocked and criticized for some of the features of BEV, but this style of communication sustains an extremely powerful in-group identity.

Social Class

Most people are uncomfortable talking about social class, but it is a reality nonetheless. All societies are differentiated; that is, there are groups and levels of society that are different and are afforded different status. *Social differentiation* is characteristic of all cultures and is simply a separation of roles and activities, a division of labor. Somebody fishes and somebody hunts; somebody delivers the mail and somebody writes books. Social *stratification* is when these differing activities and behaviors are ranked relative to one another. There is no stratification if the fisherman and the hunter are considered of equal status and importance. But if the fisherman is considered "better" than the hunter, or the author better than the mailperson, if one of these two positions is afforded more respect, money, honor, and status, then the society is stratified and there is a social-class system.

There are many issues that pertain to the study of social classes (see Hurst, 1992), but the role of language and communication is the most important. It is possible to show that certain language variants are associated with the classes. A well-known study by Labov (1972) combined pronunciation differences with place of occupation in New York City. The researchers went to Saks (high status), Macy's (middle status), and Klein's (low status) and asked sales people questions that elicited the response "fourth floor." Labov theorized that the pronunciation of the /r/ sound after a vowel (postvocalic /r/) would vary among status positions such that there would be fewer /r/ sounds in the lower class situations (e.g., "flooah" rather than "floor") and more pronounced /r/ in the upper class situations. The pattern was clear and in the expected directions. So, this single sound was able to sharply differentiate among speakers and class standing.

There are other speech sounds that vary with social class and education. Some of these are highly reliable, and situations and relationships influence others. Dropping the /g/ sound at the end of words such as "walking" and "going" (*walkin'* and *goin'*) are indications of less education and lower classes. In England, dropping an /h/ which produces '*orse* for "horse" and '*ouse* for "house" is associated with the lower classes.

One does not just fall into being a member of a social class. Members of a culture are socialized into a class system that reflects their economic, intellectual, and aesthetic experiences. People develop what are called *communication codes*. It is best to think of class codes as a collection of strategies and interpretive procedures for both the class-based use of language and interpretation of language. Class is "marked" in the sociolinguistic sense. Codes reflect the language user as a member of society with various social experiences, class being a fundamental one. Individuals have subjectively organized their reality and these concepts are central to the production and interpretation of language. When an individual in a social world that includes a class standing forms a subjective concept about some aspect of reality, there is a sign relation between the concept and the semantic reality that the concept represents. These subjective concepts are organized semiotically and systems of these concepts are codes. These systems of concepts (codes) are capable of evolution and development, but they can also remain stable.

For example, there is a well-known study by Willis (1977), who studied how young working-class men developed a subjective meaning for the concept "school." The concept "school" formed a sign relation with other various meanings such that "school" pointed to semantic categories about "resentment," "waste of time," and "conflicting authority," and these young men entered into an oppositional relation with the schools and their authority structures. This attitude is part of their class code that sees school as an obstruction that offers them little rather than a code that contained more positive signs for education. These codes develop from various symbolic contexts, including interpersonal, family, and economic environments. The students regularly encountered the educational authorities and developed communication practices that expressed their resentment. They would misbehave, fidget, make jokes, slouch in their chairs, and perform mock insubordination. They also expressed many class-specific meanings in their interactions with the authorities. The important conclusion here is that these young men do not simply reflect a class consciousness and reproduce their own class processes. They do more than that by producing and interpreting meanings across classes. Their own code is devalued, not because it is so deficient but because of prevailing institutional attitudes.

Ethnicity

Ethnicity is another social category that significantly influences communication and has interesting correlations with language use. It is difficult to define ethnicity perfectly, but some clarification is in order. First, an ethnic group must *believe* that their members share interests. They must have some collective sense of goals and commonalties. Second, the people in an ethnic group must *recognize their membership* in the group. Usually they will have learned the ways of the group early and deeply such that they know who belongs and who does not. Third, ethnic groups are keenly aware of *who is "in" and who is "out."* This is the essence of social identity that is based on the recognition of similarity and difference. The fourth quality—and an important one—of ethnic groups is that they share patterns of communication and language use.

All groups have an ethnolinguistic identity. The term *ethnolinguistic identity* is associated with the work of Giles and Johnson (1987) and refers to the psychological and social representations that language performs with respect to ethnicity. Ethnolinguistic identity is focused on interpersonal encounters and how ethnic identity and language interact to account for intercultural communication and "communication breakdowns" (Gudykunst & Ting-Toomey, 1990). How individuals use language and communication to maintain distinctiveness is a central theme in ethnolinguistic identity theory. These include linguistic markers (lexical, grammatical, and rhetorical) that establish individual and social distinctiveness.

By way of example, the speech and communication patterns of African Americans is known as Black English Vernacular (BEV). It is a social dialect that crosses regional boundaries and serves an important ethnic function for African Americans. When a group experiences isolation and discrimination such as that experienced by African Americans, they develop language patterns that are particularly marked. Typically, minority groups have their language negatively evaluated; that is, the dominant group considers it inferior.

One example of this from BEV is the absence of the verb "to be." Sentences such as "You fine" or "They mine" require the verb "are" in English ("You *are* fine," "They *are* mine"), but it is typically absent in BEV. There is a tendency to conclude that this is "bad" English, when in fact, this is the result of historical language contact and similar to some other languages that do not use the copula. Another example is the tendency for BEV to insert "be" in sentences such as "He be cool." But this is part of the aspect system (tense system) and is simply a linguistic structure that indicates habitual action. The person is not only "cool" now, he is always cool. The point is that this sort of language use is not necessarily inferior; it is simply different.

Gender

The matter of differences between men and women has been a topic of research and controversy for some time. Anthropologists studying other cultures always notice differences in the rules that characterize men's speech versus women's, but explaining these differences is difficult. Sometimes the sex of the *speaker* determines language use because of the speaker's individual nature or position in a culture. Other times, the sex of the hearer determines language use because of the relationship between the speaker and hearer. And there are times when both the speaker and the hearer are important. For example, women speaking to women change their language and communication patterns from when they are speaking to men.

One of the most commonly reported language patterns that distinguish men and women is the tendency for women to use language that is considered "more correct." In other words, men vary their language more and use more nonstandard forms. Men show a preference for more slang and less acceptable patterns of speech (cf. Milroy, 1980). There are plenty of exceptions to this rule, so one should be cautious. The influences of context, social class, relationships, and communicative goals are always very important. Skeggs (1997), for example, explained how lower class women communicate more like men, even though they guard against being stigmatized as sexual.

One of the explanations for this gender pattern is that women compensate for the status distinctions that are denied them in other aspects of life. Men are awarded status through occupation and earning power, so women compensate through speech. Moreover, women are judged by their appearance more than men are, and language is part of how you "appear." A more popular current explanation for this difference between men and women is *network strength* (Milroy, 1980). Network strength is the measure of the social ties that one has. If you mostly communicate with a limited number of people whom you know well, then you have network strength; that is, you are engaged in a recurring, well-understood, and predictable set of relationships that do not change much. It turns out that men have greater network strength. Women engage in a greater variety and diversity of relationships. They are more tolerant of differences and are willing to establish relationships on that basis. Therefore, women maintain more of a standard language use, whereas men develop a more "in crowd" with idiosyncratic usage. These differences are especially true of working-class environments.

The relation between ideology and language was underscored by Lakoff's (1975) analysis of how language by and about women influenced attitudes about women. She argued that women were not encouraged to express themselves strongly, typically expressed uncertainty, and often used language that suggested triviality. For example, a women is more likely to say "oh dear" or "darn" instead of "shit." This contributes, according to Lakoff, to a sense of submissiveness and fewer opportunities for women to express individuality.

A women's use of *tag questions* is probably the most well-known syntactic feature of women's speech pointed out by Lakoff. A tag question is attached to the end of a statement by selecting the appropriate pronoun for the subject and turning it into a question. Examples 9 and 10 are examples of tag questions:

9. I thought it was a good movie, *didn't you?*

10. He is pretty nice, don't *ya think?*

These tag questions ask the listener to confirm the speaker, and also indicate that the speaker is not fully confident in what she is saying. Overuse of tag questions indicates an insecurity and lack of individuality.

Lakoff (1975) also explained how terms used to describe women were discriminatory and indicated that their identity was overdetermined by their gender. For example, a man is always "Mr." But women can be "Mrs.," "Miss," or "Ms," depending on their marital state or identity preference. A woman is often described as a "widow" after her husband dies, but it is odd to hear a man described as a "widower." According to Lakoff, this is because a women acquires her identity through her relationship to a man, whereas a man acquires his from what are considered the more serious aspects of life.

Lakoff stimulated considerable subsequent research, and many of her conclusions have been modified. It is more commonly accepted that tag questions result from contexts in which the speaker is insecure, and women just happen to be in more of those situations. The number of tag questions used by men increases when men are in insecure and less comfortable situations. The "style" of speaking described by Lakoff is now more likely to be described as a "powerless" style than as a gender-related one. Language users increase their tag questions and the sense of insecurity about their speech when they are in powerless situations. The fact that women are simply in such situations more often explains why they exhibit the language features described by Lakoff.

Sociolinguistics is an interesting and important aspect of the entire study of language and communication. It is theoretically sophisticated and highly practical. Language is a clear mirror into the mind, and knowledge of the relations between language and society helps one understand people and cultures. Sociolinguists have worked hard to apply their craft to many problems of everyday life. Perhaps their most important contributions have been in the area of language arts in the educational environment. Children spend many years establishing language patterns before they begin school. Sometimes they arrive with linguistic deficits that interfere with learning. Sociolinguists have been instrumental in identifying and correcting these problems.

The differences between the spoken language of people from certain groups (e.g., minority groups) and the structure of the more educated formal written language that appears in textbooks has been another area of concern for sociolinguists. Some experts proposed presenting early reading material to children in the dialect of their group. Because these dialects are almost always nonstandard and stigmatized, this was a very controversial suggestion. It met with so much resistance—and failed to prove itself effective—that such approaches no longer have support. But sociolinguists have been successful at pointing out the relation between educated language use and spoken dialect, and have been helpful in designing curriculums that meet student needs.

Sociolinguists, discourse analysts, and communication scholars have had some bright successes in the interactions of language and cultural issues, legal matters, and the medical profession. Some work by Labov (1972) and Heath (1983) has been exemplary with respect to identifying the literacy problems for urban Blacks or the rural poor. There are often culture clashes between schools and communication, and language scholars have been helpful at ameliorating these tensions. It is simply not possible to study language and communication without considering the impact on society. Communication scholars continue to make progress exploring these relations.

References

Akmajian, A., Demers, R. A., and Harnish, R. M. (1980). *Linguistics: An introduction to language and communication.* Cambridge, MA: MIT Press.

Anderson, A., Garrod, S. C., & Sanford, A. J. (1983). The accessibility of pronominal antecedents as a function of episode shifts in narrative text. *Quarterly Journal of Experimental Psychology, 35A,* 427–440.

Atkinson, J. M., & Drew, P. (1979). *Order in court: The organisation of verbal interaction in judicial settings.* Atlantic Highlands, NJ: Humanities.

Austin, J. (1962). *How to do things with words.* New York: Oxford University Press.

Bach, K., & Harnish, R. M. (1979). *Linguistic communication and speech acts.* Cambridge, MA: MIT Press.

Badzinski, D. M. (1991). Children's cognitive representations of discourse: Effects of vocal cues on test comprehension. *Communication Research, 18,* 715–736.

Badzinski, D. M., & Gill, M. M. (1994). Discourse features and message comprehension. In S. A. Deetz (Ed.), *Communication yearbook 17* (pp. 301–332). Thousand Oaks, CA: Sage.

Bartlett, F. C. (1932). *Remembering: A study in experimental and social psychology.* Cambridge: Cambridge University Press.

Berlin, B., & Kay, P. (1969). *Basic color terms: Their universality and evolution.* Berkeley: University of California Press.

Bickerton, D. (1981). *The roots of language.* Ann Arbor, MI: Karoma.

Bloomfield, L. (1933). *Language.* New York: Henry Holt.

Bower, G. H., & Cirilo, R. K. (1985). Cognitive psychology and text processing. In T. A. van Dijk (Ed.), *Handbook of discourse analysis: Vol 1* (pp. 71–105). New York: Academic Press.

Bransford, J. D., & Johnson, M. K. (1973). Consideration of some problems of comprehension. In W. G. Chase (Ed.), *Visual information processing* (pp. 393–427). New York: Academic Press.

Brown, G., & Yule, G. (1983). *Discourse analysis.* Cambridge, England: Cambridge University Press.

Cassirer, E. (1944). *Essay on man. An introduction to a philosophy of human culture.* New Haven, CT: Yale University Press.

Chomsky, N. (1957). *Syntactic structures.* The Hague: Mouton.

Chomsky, N. (1965). *Aspects of a theory of syntax.* Cambridge, MA: MIT Press.

Chomsky, N. (1966). *Cartesian linguistics.* New York: Harper & Row.

Chomsky, N. (1975). *Reflections on language.* New York: Pantheon.

Cicourel, A. (1973). *Cognitive sociology: Language and meaning in social interaction.* London: Cox & Wyman.

Clark, H. H., & Clark, E. V. (1968). Semantic distinctions and memory for complex sentences. *Quarterly Journal of Experimental Psychology, 20,* 129–138.

Clark, H. H., & French, J. W. (1981). Telephone goodbyes. *Language in Society, 10,* 1–19.

Coulthard, M. (1985). *An introduction to discourse analysis.* New York: Longman.

Coulthard, R. M., & Montgomery, M. M. (Eds.). (1981). *Studies in discourse analysis.* London: Routledge & Kegan Paul.

Daniels, H. A. (1983). *Famous last words: The American language crisis reconsidered.* Carbondale: Southern Illinois University Press.

de Beaugrande, R., & Dressler, W. U. (1981). *Introduction to text linguistics.* London: Longman.

de Saussure, F. (1959). *Course in general linguistics* (Wade Baskin, Trans.). New York: Philosophical Library.

De Stefano, J. (1984). Learning to communicate in the classroom. In A. Pellegrini & T. Yawkey (Eds.), *Advances in discourse processes: Vol. 13. The development of oral and written language in social contexts* (pp. 137–163). Norwood, NJ: Ablex.

Dummett, M. (1976). What is a theory of meaning? (II). In G. Evans & J. McDowell (Eds.), *Truth and meaning* (pp. 67–137). Oxford, England: Clarendon.

Duncan, S. (1973). Toward a grammar for dyadic conversation. *Semiotica, 9,* 29–46.

Duncan, S. (1974). On the structure of speaker-auditor interaction during speaking turns. *Language in Society, 3,* 161–180.

Edmondson, W. J. (1981). Illocutionary verbs, illocutionary acts, and conversational behavior. In H. Eikmeyer & H. Reiser (Eds.), *Words, worlds, and contexts* (pp. 171–186). Berlin, Germany: Walter de Gruyter.

Ellis, D. G. (1995). Fixing communicative meaning: A coherentist theory. *Communication Research, 22,* 515–544.

Ellis, D. G., Duran, R., & Kelly, L. (1994). Discourse strategies of competent communicators: Selected cohesive and linguistic devices. *Research in Language and Social Interaction, 27,* 145–170.

Ellis, D. G., Hamilton, M., & Aho, L. (1983). Some issues in conversation coherence. *Human Communication Research, 9,* 267–282.

Fries, C. (1964). *Linguistics and reading.* New York: Holt, Rinehart & Winston.

Gardner, H. (1985). *Frames of mind.* New York: Basic Books.

Gazdar, G. J. M. (1979). *Pragmatics: Implicature, presupposition, and logical form.* New York: Academic Press.

Gazdar, G. J. M. (1981). Speech act assignment. In A. K. Joshi, B. L. Webber, & I. A. Sag (Eds.), *Elements of discourse understanding* (pp. 21–96). Cambridge, England: Cambridge University Press.

Geertz, C. (1972). *The interpretation of cultures.* New York: Basic Books.

Giles, H., & Johnson, P. (1987). Ethnolinguistic identity theory: A social psychological approach to language maintenance. *International Journal of the Sociology of Language, 68,* 69–91.

Gold, D. (1989). A sketch of the linguistic situation in Israel today. *Language in Society, 18,* 361–388.

Goodwin, C., & Duranti, A. (1992). Rethinking context: An introduction. In A. Duranti & C. Goodwin (Eds.), *Rethinking context: Language as an interactive phenomena* (pp. 1–42). Cambridge, England: Cambridge University Press.

Gough, P. B. (1965). Grammatical transformations and speed of understanding. *Journal of Verbal Learning and Verbal Behavior, 4,* 107–111.

Grice, H. P. (1975). Logic and conversation. In P. Cole & J. L. Morgan (Eds.), *Syntax and semantics 3: Speech acts* (pp. 46–58). New York: Seminar Press.

Grice, H. P. (1978). Further notes on logic and conversation. In P. Cole (Ed.), *Syntax and semantics 9: Pragmatics*. New York: Academic Press.

Gudykunst, W. B., & Ting-Toomey, S. (1990). Ethnic identity, language and communication breakdowns. In H. Giles & W. P. Robinson (Eds.), *Handbook of language and social psychology* (pp. 309–327). New York: John Wiley & Sons.

Halliday, M. A. K. (1978). *Language as social semiotic.* London: Edward Arnold.

Halliday, M. A. K., & Hasan, R. (1976). *Cohesion in English.* London: Longman.

Heath, S. B. (1983). *Ways with words.* Cambridge, England: Cambridge University Press.

Heritage, J. (1984). A change-of-state token and aspects of its sequential placement. In J. M. Atkinson & J. Heritage (Eds.), *Structures of social interaction* (pp. 299–345). Cambridge, England: Cambridge University Press.

Hockett, C. (1960). The origin of speech. *Scientific American, 203,* 88–96.

Hopper, R. (1989). Sequential ambiguity in telephone openings: 'What are you doin.' *Communication Monographs, 56,* 240–252.

Hurst, C. E. (1992). *Social inequality.* Boston: Allyn & Bacon.

Hymes, D. (1974). *Foundations in sociolinguistics.* Philadelphia: University of Pennsylvania Press.

Jacobs, S., & Jackson, S. (1983). Speech act structure in conversation: Rational aspects of pragmatic coherence. In R. T. Craig & K. Tracy (Eds.), *Conversational coherence: Form structure and strategy* (pp. 47–66). Beverly Hills, CA: Sage.

Jefferson, G. (1972). Side sequences. In D. Sudnow (Ed.), *Studies in social interaction* (pp. 294–338). New York: The Free Press.

Jespersen, O. (1922). *Language: Its nature, development and origin.* London: Allen & Unwin.

Johnson-Laird, P. N. (1969). On understanding logically complex sentences. *Quarterly Journal of Experimental Psychology, 21,* 1–13.

Johnston, J. R. (1985). The discourse symptoms of developmental disorders. In T. van Dijk (Ed.), *Handbook of discourse analysis* (Vol. 3, pp. 79–93). New York: Academic Press.

Kasher, A. (1985). Philosophy and discourse analysis. In T. van Dijk (Ed.), *Handbook of discourse analysis* (Vol. 1, pp. 231–248). New York: Academic Press.

Katz, J. J., & Fodor, J. A. (1963). The structure of a semantic theory. *Language, 39,* 170–210.

Kaufer, D. (1979). The competence/performance distinction in linguistic theory. *Philosophy of the Social Sciences, 9,* 257–275.

Kellermann, K. (1991). The conversation MOP: II. Progress through scenes in discourse. *Human Communication Research, 17,* 385–414.

Kellermann, K., Broetzman, S., Lim, T.-S., & Kitao, K. (1989). The conversation MOP: Scenes in the stream of discourse. *Discourse Processes, 12,* 27–61.

Kintsch, W., & Greene, E. (1978). The role of culture-specific schemata in the comprehension of recall of stories. *Discourse Processes, 1,* 1–13.

Kreckel, M. (1981). *Communicative acts and shared knowledge in natural discourse.* New York: Academic Press.

Kripke, S. A. (1963). Semantical considerations on modal logic. *Acta Philosophica Fennica, 16,* 323–339.

Labov, W. (1972). *Sociolinguistic patterns.* Philadelphia: University of Pennsylvania Press.

Labov, W., & Fanshel, D. (1977). *Therapeutic discourse.* New York: Academic Press.

Lakoff, R. (1975). *Language and women's place.* New York: Harper & Row.

Langacker, R. W. (1973). *Language and its structure: Some fundamental linguistic concepts.* New York: Harcourt, Brace & World.

Langer, S. (1942). *Philosophy in a new key: A study in the symbolism of reason, rite, and art.* Cambridge, MA: Harvard University Press.

Levinson, S. C. (1981). Some pre-observations on the modelling of dialogue. *Discourse Processes, 4*, 93–110.

Liles, B. L. (1971). *An introductory transformational grammar.* New York: Prentice-Hall.

Lorch, E. P., Bellack, D. R., & Augsbach, H. (1987). Young children's memory for televised stories: Effects of importance. *Child Development, 58*, 453–463.

Lyons, J. (1969). *Introduction to theoretical linguistics.* Cambridge, England: Cambridge University Press.

Matoesian, G. M. (1993). *Reproducing rape: Domination through talk in the courtroom.* Chicago: University of Chicago Press.

McNeill, D., & McNeill, N. B. (1968). What does a child mean when he says "no"? In E. M. Zale (Ed.), *Language and language behavior* (pp. 51–62). New York: Appleton-Century-Crofts.

Miller, G. A., & McKean, K. E. (1964). A chronometric study of some relations between sentences. *Quarterly Journal of Experimental Psychology, 16*, 297–308.

Milroy, L. (1980). *Language and social networks.* Oxford, England: Basil Blackwell.

Murphy, G. L. (1985). Psychological explanations of deep and surface anaphora. *Journal of Pragmatics, 9*, 785–813.

Nofsinger, R. E. (1975). The demand ticket: A conversational device for getting the floor. *Speech Monographs, 42*, 1–9.

Olson, D. R. (1970). *Cognitive development.* New York: Academic Press.

Penfield, W. (1966). Speech, perception and the uncommitted cortex. In J. C. Eccles (Ed.), *Brain and conscious experience* (pp. 217–237). New York: Springer-Verlag.

Piaget, J. (1950). *The language and thought of the child.* London: Routledge & Kegan Paul.

Planalp, S., & Tracy, K. (1980). Not to change the topic but . . . : A cognitive approach to the study of conversation. In D. Nimmo (Ed.), *Communication yearbook 4* (pp. 237–258). New Brunswick, NJ: Transaction.

Pomerantz, A. (1978). Compliment responses: Notes on the co-operation of multiple constraints. In J. Schenkein (Eds.), *Studies in the organization of conversational interaction* (pp. 79–112). New York: Academic Press.

Pomerantz, A., & Fehr, B. J. (1997). Conversation analysis: An approach to the study of social action as sense making practices. In T. A. van Dijk (Ed.), *Discourse as social interaction* (pp. 64–91). Thousand Oaks, CA: Sage.

Posner, R. (1980). Semantics and pragmatics of sentence connectives in natural language. In J. Searle, F. Kiefer, & M. Bierwisch (Eds.), *Speech act theory and pragmatics* (pp. 169–204). Dordrecht, Netherlands: Reidel.

Robbins, R. H. (1967). *A short history of linguistics.* Bloomington: Indiana University Press.

Rosaldo, M. (1982). The things we do with words: Ilongot speech acts and speech act theory in philosophy. *Language in Society, 11*, 203–237.

Rumelhart, D. E. (1980). Schemata: The building blocks of cognition. In R. J. Spiro, B. C. Bruce, & W. F. Brewer (Eds.), *Theoretical issues in reading comprehension: Perspectives from cognitive psychology, linguistics, artificial intelligence* (pp. 61–83). Hillsdale, NJ: Lawrence Erlbaum Associates.

Sachs, J. S. (1967). Recognition memory for syntactic and semantic aspects of connected discourse. *Perception and Psychophysics, 2*, 437–442.

Sacks, H. (1973). *Lectures at summer linguistic institute.* Ann Arbor: University of Michigan.

Sacks, H., & Schegloff, E. A. (1979). Two preferences in the organization of reference to persons in conversation and their interaction. In G. Psathas (Ed.), *Everyday language: Studies in ethnomethodology* (pp. 15–21). New York: Irvington.

Sacks, H., Schegloff, E. A., & Jefferson, G. (1974). A simplest systematics for the organization of turn-taking for conversation. *Language, 50*, 696–735.

Sag, I., & Hankamer, J. (1984). Toward a theory of anaphoric processing. *Linguistics and Philosophy, 7*, 325–345.

Sanders, R. E. (1981). The interpretation of discourse. *Communication Quarterly, 29*, 209–217.

Sanders, R. E. (1987). *Cognitive foundations of calculated speech*. Albany: State University of New York Press.

Sanford, A. J., & Garrod, S. C. (1981). *Understanding written language: Explorations in comprehension beyond the sentence*. Chichester, England: Wiley.

Schank, R. C. (1973). Identification of conceptualizations underlying natural language. In R. C. Schank & K. M. Colby (Eds.), *Computer models of thought and language* (pp. 16–39). San Francisco: Freeman.

Schank, R. C., & Ableson, R. (1977). *Scripts, plans, goals, and understanding*. Hillsdale, NJ: Lawrence Erlbaum Associates.

Schank, R. C., & Burstein, M. (1985). Artificial intelligence: Modeling memory for language understanding. In T. van Dijk (Ed.), *Handbook of discourse analysis* (Vol. 1, pp. 145–166). New York: Academic Press.

Schegloff, E. A. (1968). Sequencing in conversational openings. *American Anthropologist, 70*, 1075–1095.

Schegloff, E. A. (1972). Sequencing in conversational openings. In J. Gumperz & D. Hymes (Eds.), *Directions in sociolinguistics* (pp. 346–380). New York: Holt, Rinehart & Winston.

Schegloff, E. A., & Sacks, H. (1973). Opening up closings. *Semiotica, 8*, 289–327.

Schiffrin, D. (1977). Opening encounters. *American Sociological Review, 42*, 679–691.

Schiffrin, D. (1994). *Approaches to discourse*. Cambridge, MA: Blackwell.

Schneider, K. P. (1988). *Small talk: Analyzing phatic discourse*. Marburg, Germany: Hitzeroth.

Scribner, S., & Cole, M. (1981). *The psychology of literacy*. Cambridge, MA: Harvard University Press.

Searle, J. R. (1969). *Speech acts: An essay in the philosophy of language*. London: Cambridge University Press.

Searle, J. R. (1974). Chomsky's revolution in linguistics. In G. Harman (Eds.), *On Noam Chomsky: Critical essays* (pp. 2–33). New York: Anchor.

Searle, J. R. (1975). Indirect speech acts. In P. Cole & J. Morgan (Eds.), *Syntax and semantics 3: Speech acts* (pp. 59–82). New York: Academic Press.

Shotter, J. (1993). *Conversational realities: Constructing life through language*. London: Sage.

Sigman, S. (1987). *A perspective on social communication*. Lexington, MA: Heath.

Sillars, M. O. (1964). Rhetoric as act. *Quarterly Journal of Speech, 50*, 277–284.

Skeggs, B. (1997). *Formations of class and gender*. Thousand Oaks, CA: Sage.

Skinner, B. F. (1957). *Verbal behavior*. New York: Appleton-Century-Crofts.

Slobin, D. (1966). Grammatical transformations in childhood and adulthood. *Journal of Verbal Learning and Verbal Behavior, 5*, 219–227.

Stubbs, M. (1983). *Discourse analysis*. Chicago: University of Chicago Press.

Sutherland, N. S. (1966). Discussion of 'Some reflections on competence and performance' by J. A. Fodor and M. F. Garrett. In J. Lyons & R. J. Wales (Eds.), *Psycholinguistic papers* (pp. 126–141). Edinburgh, Scotland: Edinburgh University Press.

Tannen, D. (Ed.). (1984). *Coherence in spoken and written discourse*. Norwood, NJ: Ablex.

Tannen, D. (1987). Repetition in conversation: Toward a poetics of talk. *Language, 63*, 574–605.

Tracy, K. (1998). Analyzing context: Framing the discussion. *Research on Language and Social Interaction, 31*, 1–28.

Tyler, L. K., & Marslen-Wilson, W. D. (1982). The resolution of discourse anaphora: Some on-line studies. *Text, 2*, 263–291.

van Dijk, T. A. (1980). *Macrostructures*. Hillsdale, NJ: Lawrence Erlbaum Associates.

van Dijk, T. A. (1985). Semantic discourse analysis. In T. A. van Dijk (Ed.), *Handbook of discourse analysis* (Vol. 2, pp. 103–136). London: Academic Press.

van Dijk, T. A. (1987). *Communicating racism*. Newbury Park, CA: Sage.

van Dijk, T. A. (1988). *News as discourse*. Newbury Park, CA: Sage.

van Dijk, T. A. (1997). Discourse as interaction in society. In T. A. van Dijk (Ed.), *Discourse as social interaction* (pp. 1–37). London: Sage.

Villaume, W. A., & Cegala, D. J. (1988). Interaction involvement and discourse strategies: The patterned use of cohesive devices in conversation. *Communication Monographs, 55,* 22–40.

Vygotsky, L. S. (1965). *Thought and language.* Cambridge, MA: MIT Press.

Watson, J. B., & Raynor, R. (1920). Conditioned emotional reactions. *Journal of Experimental Psychology, 3,* 1–14.

Whorf, B. L. (1956). Languages and logic. In J. B. Carroll (Ed.), *Language, thought, and reality: Selected writings* (pp. 39–54). Cambridge: MIT Press.

Wilensky, R. (1981). PAM. In R. C. Schank & C. K. Reisbeck (Eds.), *Inside computer understanding: Five programs plus miniatures* (pp. 136–179). Hillsdale, NJ: Lawrence Erlbaum Associates.

Willis, P. (1977). *Learning to labor: How working class kids get working class jobs.* Farnbrough, England: Saxon House.

Author Index

Subject Index